KOREA OF THE JAPANESE

BY THE SAME AUTHOR

THE SCHOONER CALIFORNIA
CURSED BE THE TREASURE
THE CHILDREN REAP
SHINJU

THE BODLEY HEAD

OLD KOREA

KOREA
OF THE JAPANESE

by

H. B. DRAKE

With twenty-four illustrations from photographs

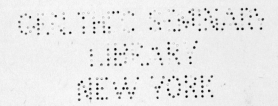
LONDON : JOHN LANE THE BODLEY HEAD LIMITED
NEW YORK : DODD, MEAD AND COMPANY

First Published in 1930

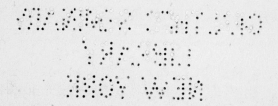

Made and Printed in Great Britain
by William Clowes and Sons, Limited, London and Beccles.

TO

J. B. STUDENY

AND

J. F. HUSS

CONTENTS

LIST OF ILLUSTRATIONS

KOREA OF THE JAPANESE

KOREA OF THE JAPANESE

I

THE LAND OF MORNING CALM

IT is inevitable in writing on Korea that one should yield for a title to the seduction of this name. It is always done. It proves at least that one has trained through the country, travelling between Japan and Manchuria, with a possible " stop off " at the capital. It links one up as a familiar with the slender band of whites who, by an amazing choice or a fantastic accident, have been marked out peculiar to live among the " Top-knots." For it is the authorized translation of Chosun, the native name.

Yet one may deliberately select it, too, for its symbolism, for its irony.

When I first announced my intention of going to Korea I set my friends hunting bookshelves for atlases, some a little sneakingly, others in unashamed confession of ignorance. It was in the Black Sea, wasn't it ? And was it spelt with a C or a K ? Well, you will find it on the map hanging helplessly from Chinese Manchuria, with a slender grip to an edge of Russian Siberia, dangling down—but with a reluctant upward curl—towards Japan.

Again, is this symbolism, or is this irony?

When, after a residence of two years, I was preparing to return to England, a trio of students, who had the sniggering manner of an illicit delegation, called upon me, and after an infinite and wearisome palaver besought me to write to the English papers and tell of the condition of their " unhappy country." They had ceased to snigger now. They were in bitter earnest. Their thick lips drooped. Their flat eyes widened. One might have said there was an incipient bristling in the straight fall of their long, black hair. I refilled my pipe, not knowing how to answer them, indeed, not knowing whether to laugh or weep. The childish misconception that underlay their appeal had in it more of the tragic than the pathetic. They leant towards me, obviously disheartened at my silence, forlorn figures in their ill-fitting uniforms of summer grey, brass-buttoned, open at the neck, displaying brown and shirtless skins.

" Please, yess," one of them repeated, " you write to Eengleesh papar, yess, ees it not so ? "

England for them was so serene, so mighty,

extending so beneficent a hand to the outcast and the oppressed, that a word from her would deliver them from their bondage, would make of their " unhappy country " once again " the land of morning calm." All that was in their minds, conceived in terms of magic wands and fairy godmothers. But I remembered my atlas-hunting friends ; and the refrain ran through my head, " Is it spelt with a C or a K ? "

What could I answer ? Besides, if I wrote at all, I wanted to tell of incredible mountains, of intense skies, of fantastic islands in transparent seas, of red-pillared temples set about with pine overpeering the ravines of granite hills, where one could bask beneath a beatific sun and commune with the Spirit of the Ancient Earth.

Well, I was as poetically remote from actuality as they. But one thing I saw clearly : the immense gap of ignorance which in spite of education, literature and travel still divides East from West. These students knew little enough of England, but England knows nothing of Korea. Yet Korea is worth knowing. It focuses so many problems, focuses them so clearly. One can study them there as though in a museum, each distinctly isolated, without irrelevant complexities, because the lines of life there are so simple. Problems political, national,

educational, problems as ephemeral as fashions
in dress and architecture, problems as fundamental as the clash of race and creed, stand out
for one in separate relief; but against a richly
human background, and in a world wild and
splendid that is the realization of romance.

One might begin where I broke off, frankly
with no solution to offer, with those earnest-
faced, brown figures forlornly uniformed in sign
of servitude to an alien despotism. It was in
1910 that Japan formally annexed Korea, and
with curious ill taste jubilantly celebrates the
anniversary each year in the subjugated country.
She does so with evident misgivings, because a
few days before the event the prisons fill with
suspected malcontents, who later are released
without accusation and without trial, having
suffered no worse than a temporary confinement in an extremely up-to-date cell, and a daily
baptism of cold water. Japan's reasons for
annexation, when officially expressed on paper,
are an exquisite parody of similar European
justifications, particularly British. She acted
entirely from unimpeachable motives. Her
altruism was sublime. Korea was shamefully
misgoverned (she was) and Japan was conscience-
bound to extend to her the benefits of modern

BY THE SEA

progress (she has). But there is an Eastern savour in this Western wind. The Korean Year Book adds that Japan and Korea are like long-separated brothers who have at last been reunited. But the only brotherly element in their relationship seems to be that they mutually refrain from marrying into one another's families. The plain fact, of course, was that Japan had no alternative. The Koreans as a people are marked down as a prey to any predatory power. Hate domination as they will, it is in their nature to be dominated. But a Russian or Chinese Korea would have been as dangerous to Japan as a German Ireland would have been to England in 1914. Japan acted in self-defence. It was quite impossible for her to have acted otherwise. And in any consideration of Korean independence one must take this as basic. But for me it would have been no sort of answer to those questioning students to say, "You are dear, delightful children. You have the most beautiful smiles in the world. But unfortunately, as the gods have seen fit to arrange terrestrial things, there is a menace in your very charm and weakness. So your long-separated elder brother is obliged to step in and order your house."

Yet that *is* the answer.

Indeed, one feels inclined to philosophize and

throw the blame on Heaven. The race is to
the swift and the battle to the strong. When the
League of Nations has developed some scheme
of International Hospitals for the feebler peoples
Korea may be returned her independence.
But her independence now would create a
vacuum which would suck in Russia like a
hurricane and China like a typhoon. Possibly
America, with another rush of wind, preaching
well-intentioned sublimities, but ineffectual for
want of a resolute backing in guns. But the
fault would not be with America. Remember
our philosophy ; it is the gods who are to blame.

I turned the subject. I put banal questions
to them. The three intent faces relaxed into
wan smiles. I asked :

" What will you do when you leave the
University ? "

Their expressions became thoughtful, which
on the Korean face has the air of a thick wall
enclosing a vacancy. The student whom I
knew best of the three, and who bore the
exquisite name of You Sea Cook (perhaps I
could spell it Yu See Kuk), began to elongate his
neck from his unbuttoned collar as a preliminary to replying.

" Always I shall study," he said.

I might have anticipated the answer, because

I had heard it before. I had travelled with Yu See Kuk. We had spent days together exploring old temples and nights together in Korean inns. I knew his ambition. He was the student of the family. His people slaved willingly on the land to maintain him in his aloof dignity. They would continue willingly to do so to the end of their days. Then he would live with his brothers. They would feed his wife and his children. And always he would study. He would read many books, squatting on the heated floor of his little room bowed over a tiny table. That was what Western education had achieved for him. He remained Eastern to the soul, but besides the Chinese Classics he would be able to read Thomas Hardy and Oscar Wilde and Galsworthy, and whoever else the succeeding divinities might be. Yet he was such a delightful boy. He told me, with the sweetest modesty, how at his return home for the vacations the whole village would meet him, coming miles along the road, bearing banners in his honour. It was a duty he owed, not merely to himself but to his people, that he should never stain his hands with labour. Always he would study.

And behind it there was no suggestion that the study might come to any serviceable fruition.

He was to sit in solitude and absorb ; but he would not be called upon to give. He would eventually die, blown full with learned air, and his memory would be revered. But, meanwhile, what of his country ?

Perhaps there was truth in the paper altruism of Japan.

" And you, Pal Sung Yi ? " I asked.

Pal Sung Yi had softly pouting lips and a very flat nose. He tilted his head a trifle, hugged a nervous knee, and replied with a delicious simplicity :

" I shall write novels."

Just as easy as that, you understand.

" Then you will need to know many people and see many things," I suggested.

His lifted brows, shaped to perfect curves above soft eyes of muddy brown, expressed a bewildered questioning.

Surely after studying for five years he would have read enough books to produce other books. Surely . . . or of what use was the University ?

That was their outlook. And these, presumably, were the cream of Korean in-telligence. They had passed a difficult com-petitive entrance examination into the University. Their uniform commanded an almost slavish respect throughout the country. But they could see no farther than books for the sake of books. One might dislike the Japs as one dislikes a governess, but one shrewdly suspected that these little children needed some one with a sharp tongue and a stick to hand if they were to be fitted to this world as the gods have planned it.

Yet somehow, by writing to the English papers, I was to alter all this. But, then, I had written books. That very day they had handled them, passing them to each other reverently, admiring their blatant coloured covers. They would like to buy them, but how much did they cost? When I told them four yen, they exclaimed " *Ai-go !* " and looked furtively to see if their hands were clean. Four yen, merely for a story. The English must be very rich if they could give four yen merely for a story. And their eyes wandering round my room declared the same respect. A perfectly vulgar room, without harmony, without proportion, set with a Daventry couch, some dilapidated chairs with carved arms and faded tapestry, a carpet folded back at one end to curb its unnecessary extent, a Japanese *kakemono* among Victorian prints and missionary calendars on the wall. It was dreadful ; but it represented wealth, luxury, splendour unimaginable to these students who lived in such hovels as one could see from the windows, clustering in curves about diminutive, foul courtyards, the thatched roofs aged to a dull purplish grey, for all the world like a cluster of mushrooms. But I belonged to a happy people. I wrote stories that cost four yen. Surely, if I would write to the English papers . . .

I turned to the third.

" And you, Gin An Siki ? "

Without the least despondency he replied :

" For me, I think, there is nothing."

" Ah, of course," I said, remembering. " You are a law student."

Gin An Siki was a law student, and for him there was nothing.

Yet that was not strictly accurate. There are openings for Korean students of law. There are even Korean judges. There may be two Korean judges on a tribunal of three ; but the third is Japanese, he is president of the court, and he has the power of absolute veto. The Koreans are not encouraged to meddle in legal matters. The governess with the sharp tongue and the stick to hand will take all needful action.

So one swung sharply round to another view. One understood the complaint of the children.

And it was always so. At least it was with me. The problem is negative, not positive. It is so easy to see where both sides are in the wrong, but not where they are in the right. One pities the Koreans, but knows them for incorrigible ineffectives ; one admits the Japanese efficiency, but dislikes its methods and applications. With the best will in the world no one can help the Koreans ; and with the best will in the world the Japanese will never learn how to help. Their arrogance, their officiousness, their bursts of injustice, their subtlety, are so much more conspicuous than their superhuman and heart-breaking endeavours to uplift a people incapable of uplift. The Koreans clamour for freedom as children clamour for a world without grown-ups. But who's to cook the dinner, and light the fires, and clean the rooms ?

But if one talks of cleaning !

The problem is best stated as a quadratic equation with two answers—plus or minus one !

You see, they are irreconcilable.

My students trod with a clumsy carefulness as they left. In their own houses they would have removed their boots before entering, and to step with dirty boots on a carpet that would have cost them two years' income was shocking to their sense of a decorous humility. But I saw them again at the station when I left the Land of

Morning Calm. They couldn't speak to me there because the teaching staff stood by in force. But as I shook them by the hand the appeal was in their eyes, like a secret that had passed between us : " You write to Eengleesh papar, yess, and tell of our unhappee countree ? "

I would take the first train back if the gods permitted, but not drawn by any sentimental pity, nor any virtuous indignation. I would go to the Diamond Mountains and climb to the Peak of the Ten Thousand Resemblances, and meditate on the stern and wonderful ways of our Mother the Earth.

THE CRYSTAL PEAK, THE DIAMOND MOUNTAINS

II

GRAVES AND FUNERALS

IT is a commonplace that the East reverses our Western processes of thought. If I want to say to the egg-vendor, " The eggs were all bad which you brought me yesterday," I must express it in the form, " Yesterday me brought eggs as for all bad were." So before one speaks of Eastern life one must speak of Eastern death.

My most particular memory of a Korean funeral is somehow entangled with a certain Mr. Poole. Or more correctly, Dr. Poole. The doctorate I surmise, because it is difficult to believe that any American engaged in educational work would be without the undistinguished distinction. Dr. Poole's exact line of education was training the Christian Young Men of China to take " pictures," or as we should say, photographs, and to play base-ball. He happened to be in Korea, because in the early summer of 1927 there had been a rather rapid exodus of missionaries from China. He was

13

lodging in the same house as myself. Within
five minutes of introduction I knew the better
part of his family history, and within ten he was
unpacking albums of " pictures " in which he
knew I should be " in'erested." As a matter of
fact, I thought I should be, but Dr. Poole's idea
of albums seemed to be like Heaven's idea of the
world. Photographs good and bad lay crowded
together without selection and without plan.
The simple fact that a picture had come into
being seemed a sufficient reason that it should
find a place. So I rapidly grew weary of
turning the pages, though arrested at times by
some astonishing type, or by some glimpse of
Chinese life so intimate that I marvelled at the
impudence which made possible such familiar
records. But when I looked at Dr. Poole I saw
that it was not impudence. His face behind
his dark-glassed, horn-rimmed goggles showed
banally inexpressive as of a man to whom the
suggestion would be merely unintelligible that
there might be a certain indelicacy in thrusting
a camera into a stranger's face and " shooting "
him because his particular stage of leprous decay
was " mighty in'eresting," or into a private
apartment where devout figures crouched
prostrate before an ancestral shrine. I thought
of myself after innumerable paradings of the

streets, camera in hand, returning home without
a film expended because of this hyper-sensitive
shrinking ; but I did not explain this to Dr.
Poole because I knew he would not understand.

Curiously enough, the immediate effect of his
albums on me was to brace me to a ruthless
rudeness. I would cast aside my absurd modesty,
and make such records too for the delectation
of my friends in England. So I took down my
camera, and slinging it to my shoulder stalked
with a determined air into the streets.

Every yard of them cried to be recorded.
Dignified white figures passed sedately by,
long-robed, stepping with a leisurely ease, bearing
upon upright heads the absurdest hats in the
world : flimsy, transparent structures of horsehair, like the ghosts of inverted flower-pots on
wide rims, uplifted from the crown by a gauze
cage protectively enclosing the hair drawn up
into a twisted top-knot. The women, also in
white, had less dignity than the men. Their
heads, mostly uncovered, showed black, oiled
hair drawn flatly back and knotted on the neck.
Their waists were bunchy from the clumsy
enfoldings of their skirts. Their breasts, dis-
coloured and unlovely, hung pendent beneath
short bodices. They strode as though in a
resolute neglect of feminine grace, with feet wide

apart, with necks erect in the manner of those accustomed to bearing burdens on their heads, the wide, loose ends of their trousers beneath their skirts giving them something of the appearance of vultures.   Children swarmed everywhere. Some were stark naked, some wore six-inch bodices beneath which their rice-filled stomachs rounded to amazing proportions. The elder children were dressed in exact counterpart of the women and the men, except that they wore no hats. They looked healthy and contented, though a scalp here and there was covered with distressing sores. They played shuttlecock, with ankles instead of bats. They played hopscotch, sturdily exact in their movements in spite of babies strapped to their backs, who slept in entire unconcern with heads drooping sideways from limp necks. They played with cards, with coins, with the refuse of the overflowing garbage-boxes, with stones, with dust, with mud.

All this I could readily have converted into pictures for albums. And the storekeepers squatting behind immense flat baskets of grain, and the sweet-sellers jangling great scissors, and the oxen loaded with fuel from the hills moving like animated stacks, and the men equally loaded looking from behind like towers of brush-wood precariously balanced on pantalooned

FUEL FROM THE HILLS

legs, and where water trickled in the open sewers the groups of washing women beating wet garments with a rattle of wooden clubs. Always and everywhere the washing women. . . . But my resolution ebbed from me. I couldn't bring myself to level a camera into these solemn and patient faces. But I told myself, of course, that the light was unsuitable. Beneath such a blinding sun, such an intense blue sky, there could be no smooth, soft play of shadows.

I wondered whether such a consideration would daunt the zeal of Dr. Poole.

Then I found the crowd suddenly thickening. Policemen on horseback appeared around a corner, bullying the road clear. I heard a sad and measured chant. A double file of banner-bearers swung into sight, with coloured streamers inscribed with characters slung from long, slender poles—a funeral.

I furtively slipped my camera from its case.

The crowd pressed back to the sides of the wide street as the procession began to pass.

Behind the banners came lanterns, unlit, long, slight constructions of papered bamboo slung like the banners from the tops of poles. An interminable succession. And then the hearse—the palanquin, rather—with a couple of figures in front, completely veiled in sackcloth, borne on

C

chairs.   The palanquin was bright with colours,
red, yellow, blue.   High above the heads of
the priests who walked beside it, it loomed like
an immense and gaudy caravan, except that its
swaying showed that it did not move on wheels.
It required forty men to carry that dead body to
its grave.   They marched in step, in front, behind,
to either side, their shoulders yoked beneath a
framework of heavy crossing beams.   And as they
marched they chanted in a falling cadence a
slow, repetitive lament.

The palanquin passed.

There followed a train of mourners, two and
two, drawn in high rickshas.   They were clothed
in sackcloth, and on their heads were peculiar
hats, also of sackcloth, but stiffened to rise sheer
from the forehead and curl over to the back,
giving the faces the appearance of ancient
Egyptians in a fresco.

The sackcloth gave place to ordinary white as
the lesser mourners appeared.   One saw an
occasional Western dress, or an Eastern robe
surmounted by a straw hat or a trilby.   And
always to either side a long string of boys and
men, in round, flat hats of black felt, bearing
bright wreaths of artificial flowers supported on
easel-like frames.

An endless, endless train.

Then suddenly another palanquin, complete with the veiled figures in front, with the priests to either side, with the mourners following, and the yoked and chanting bearers. But this was no second funeral. The first was make-believe, to cheat the evil spirits who are always on watch to do harm to a man treading the dark and unknown way. The real corpse was in the second palanquin, the real procession had only just begun.

There was no sign of sorrow. The hired men who carried wreaths and banners looked about them with complete indifference. The mourners on their rickshas were stolidly complacent as though hardly aware even that they were on view. The chanting of the palanquin-bearers came to sound less like a lament than a cadence to keep them in step. And it lengthened seemingly to miles.

But when it had all passed by, straggling into an indiscriminate rabble of street followers, I found my unused camera still dangling from my hand.

The crowd about me set into a rapid chatter of expressive gutturals, forming into knots to discuss the wonderful affair. That must have been a very, very rich man. The white-robed crowd! I remembered the significance of that ever-present white. It was the Korean colour of mourning, adopted long ago as the everyday dress because Korean custom prescribed such an extended period of mourning that it was simpler always to wear white.

On New Year's Day the children might wear bright greens and reds, but the men and the women robed themselves daily in the livery of death.

I turned away from the streets—it really *was* hot—and in a few steps was on the hills. I rested on a granite rock within the shadow of a clump of twisted pines. Just below me on the slope the ground was mounded into little humps, grass-covered, with a foot-worn track threading up between. These were the dead, without flowers, without tablets, with no enclosing wall ; yet they ruled the land. They lay there as though with huddled-up knees, like discarded corpses after a battle, with the grass spread over them like a blanket. But no grave was forgotten. Once a year the living kinsfolk would come and scrape the earth bare and strew dust, and a man would rather have no one to feed him while alive than no one to do him such a reverence when dead.

Looking out across a valley I could see a cleared space on a further wooded hill. There

was a solitary grave there, more imposing, more
splendid. These were the poor, but that, I had
been told, was the grave of a certain Lady An,
an emperor's concubine. She lay beneath an
immense dome of earth, surrounded with
guardian images, protected on three sides by a
roofed wall, and set in front with a massive
altar stone. It stood well up the slope,
approached at the foot by a gate of posts like a
football goal, faced by a shrine, and with a
caretaker's lodge to one side. She was well
provided for, Lady An.

Her grave was an exact model, though in
miniature, of other royal tombs. Always the
enormous mound of earth, the images, the altar,
and the wall.

One met these tombs at every turn. Tombs
of the humble, tombs of the great. Magnificent
trees grew about them, as about the monasteries
and temples, in a country otherwise denuded of
timber. Around the villages, above the rice-
fields, the hill-sides came out in sporadic humps,
singly or in clusters, as though from some curious
disease of earth. Usually on waste land ; but
sometimes one saw a grave in the middle of a
paddy, and to that there would be some
interesting tale.

The site is all-important. You must hold a

solemn feast, and pay a witch-dancer to select a
situation for the grave.   If she chooses to select
it, possibly through august divination, possibly
through spite, in the middle of your neighbour's
field, he has no choice, if he is a wise man, but to
sell you his land, or, if he is foolish and refuses to
sell, to wake up some morning and find that a
grave had grown there in the night.   For bury
your dead there you must.   You have no option.
To bury him elsewhere would mean a life of
haunting ill-fortune.   But judging by the usual
lie of graves the witch-dancer does not frequently
indulge in such freaks of spite.

Later I was to travel with Yu See Kuk to the
old capital of Kyung Ju.   I found it a land of
graves.   They grew, not in mounds, but in
hills, altering the configuration of the country.
The dwindled city lay in a welter of stones, but
the tombs remained.   From the tops of them one
looked down as though from a tower on to
the miserable hovels of the living.   Diminutive
figures moved there at their ephemeral tasks ; but
the dead overpeered them, overawed them.

Yet the Japanese are altering all that.   The
tombs are being opened.   Their treasures stand
classified and labelled on the shelves of museums.
But do the dead take no revenge ?

You will still find a man, when fortune is

THE ROYAL TOMBS, KYUNG JU

against him, taking counsel with the witch-dancer, and shifting his father's grave to a more propitious site ; for if misfortune does not grow from the anger of the dead it has no meaning. And for the same reason a funeral is a costly matter. Every honour must be paid to appease the departed, though the living go into debt for it, a debt piled up from generation to generation, of which those vast tombs might be a symbol.

Quite apart from superstition, from cramping custom and paralysing fear, speaking in mere terms of money the dead hold the living in a strangle grip.

Possibly this is the secret of Korea.

When I returned home that evening I was greeted effusively by Dr. Poole. He had been out with his camera too, a blatant and conspicuous affair—though probably most efficient—which you held up to your eyes to bring it the more effectively to bear upon your object. He had had a most successful time. He had " gotten pictures of most everything " : the store-keepers, the sweet-vendors, the loaded oxen, the loaded men, the washing women.

He had been " almighty fortunate." He had seen a funeral, " quite a swell parade."

He showed me the photographs a few days later. There were several of the funeral, but one in particular, showing the palanquin at a tilt, a block of shadow against a dead white sky, the foreground blurred by the top of an unfocused flower-pot hat. It was entirely without atmosphere, crude in its heavy contrast of tones. It revealed nothing.

Yet I became quite friendly with Dr. Poole, in an amiable, superficial way. He had many excellent human qualities. He told me that it had distressed him when he first went to China to find that the young men held aloof from baseball. They considered such exercise only fit for coolies. But he was persuading them.

Precisely why do people like Dr. Poole come East?

AS SEEN FROM THE GRAVE-TOPS

III

THE EMPEROR'S PORTRAIT

IT arrived in a car guarded by policemen. We were drawn up two deep to either side of the school drive, professors and students, reaching from the gateway to the porch. It was a cold day, but the occasion being august, coats and hats were not permitted. We were like soldiers on parade standing at ease on wait for the colonel. The drill major, resplendent in tight blue uniform gaudy with scarlet and gold, kept watch down the road for the coming of the car. His long sword flapping against his short bandy leg seemed to irritate him like an importunate dog. The Director (or as we should say, the Principal or the Head) stood stiffly by the gate, uneasily clad in evening dress in violent disregard of the hour. He was a diminutive figure, and he carried his apparel in the manner of a tailor's dummy, with legs a little apart and arms hanging out from the body. The illusion would have been complete if he had not from time to time put up a nervous

white-gloved hand to finger at his bow, which
fell limply forward well below his collar stud,
and threatened momently to slip apart in
despairing exhaustion. Also he wore a white
flower in his buttonhole, his cuffs protruded
magnificently, and his trousers fell well over his
shoes.

The announcement that the portrait was to
arrive that morning revealed to me suddenly a
curious misconception into which I had fallen.
During the school year there were many occasions
when we gathered to celebrate divine events.
For instance, the birthday of the reigning
Emperor, the birthday of the Emperor Meiji who
had created modern Japan, the birthday of the
Emperor Jimmu Tenno (I was always terrified
lest I should inadvertently refer to him by the
disrespectful diminutive of Jimmy) who came
down from heaven seven hundred years before
Christ and founded the Japanese imperial line
unbroken to this day. Also there was New
Year, and odds and ends of festivals like that.
The celebrations always took exactly the same
form. We gathered in the school hall, sang
the national anthem, bowed to the Emperor's
portrait, listened to a harangue by the Director,
and retired—the staff at least—to a room apart
to eat oranges and seaweed and rice and cuttle-

fish and drink *saké*. At least, I thought we used to bow to the Emperor's portrait, because I knew that was what we were meant to do. We certainly bowed, and before doing so were turned, at a command from the drill major, half left, which brought us facing the door of a corner cupboard in the hall. It seems to me still quite natural that I should assume that the cupboard contained the portrait, not knowing that the portrait had not yet arrived, and having heard so many stories of its reverend and inviolable nature. Certainly it had seemed a trifle odd to bow to the door of a closed cupboard which guarded an image too divine to gaze upon, but no odder than other things one was called upon to do in Korea and Japan. But the coming of the portrait shattered that amusing misconception. We had bowed, not to a cupboard, but to Kyoto.

I have an idea that you are laughing at me. But let me explain that the portrait, of which every school possesses a copy, is held in such respect that there have been many mortalities among teachers who have rushed into blazing buildings to rescue it from the flames. And if you wish to ruin a Director's career—he may be your personal enemy, or you may covet his position—you have merely to damage the

Emperor's portrait, and his occupation is gone.
If he is high-minded and of the ancient breed he
will write letters to his friends explaining his
conduct and cut his stomach open with a sharp
knife in an exact and prescribed fashion. If he
is low-minded and of the modern breed he will
simply resign.

While speaking of those ceremonies let me
enlarge upon them a little more fully. The
school hall was a well-proportioned and ample
chamber which held the three hundred and fifty
students commodiously, with the staff, perhaps
forty of us, seated down the sides. At one end
was a platform, set with a table in front and a
table behind. In the back wall was a large,
shallow alcove, shuttered, and screened behind
the shutters with drawing curtains. It was here
that the portrait, after its arrival, was installed,
between two scrolls each inscribed with a single
character, brushed on with magnificent, bold
strokes. You might translate them tamely
as Loyalty and Piety. Piety of Virgilian
significance. Indeed, to understand the terms
fully would be to understand the whole ethic of
Japan. Loyalty to the Emperor, blind, ardent
and unswerving, through life, into death, beyond
death. Piety—that is, reverence for one's parents,
for one's ancestors, equally blind, ardent and

unswerving, rooting the nation in an unshakable
antiquity, vitalizing it with a single purpose.
That at least is the theory.

Beside the platform was the cupboard of the
amusing misconception. Yet it had its use.

Well dressed for these occasions, the students in
their customary uniforms, the teachers in morning
coats, in frock coats, in evening dress, the last
being the consummation of etiquette. But the
tiny Japanese home affords little space for the
storing of such apparel. The teachers would
appear in creased garments, smelling of moth-
balls, as though dragged hastily from a school
acting-cupboard. For the most part they preferred flimsy materials, shiny black cottons, so
that their long-tailed coats hung about them like
artists' aprons. I used to laugh at their unconscious incongruity when describing it to my
friends but really I was less sensitive to its
humour than its pathos. It would have been
so much more seemly if they had dressed in
their native robes. They knew how to wear
them. Skirted, with wide sleeves, their necks
free, they would have been in harmony with the
spirit of the celebrations, with their rather
fierce, intensely purposeful, devotion of the
Yamato Damashii, the Soul of Old Japan. As it
was, one wondered just how much of all this

they sincerely believed. What did those characters of stupendous import really convey to
them ? Was their singing an unmeaning repetition, their bowing a formal pose ?

The ritual never varied. As the Director
entered the hall the resplendent drill major
called us sharply to our feet, " *Kirits !* " * called
us sharply to bow, " *Ré !* " We bowed in unison,
the Director returning the salute with a lesser
inclination. Then he faced the still-veiled
portrait, not yet ascending to the platform. The
curtains opened. We were in the Presence.
We bowed in a hushed awe.

When the portrait was again veiled the drill
major called, " One, two, three ! " and the whole
assembly broke into the national anthem. But
there was no one to give the note. At first
there was a deafening and indistinguishable
roar, without melody, without key. A teacher
to the right sang in a high tenor, a teacher to
the left sang in a deep bass. But gradually the
more powerful voices drew the singing into
unison as though by a kind of vocal magnetism.
The anthem ended in some sort of concord.

As for me, I could not join in the strange words.
I watched the Korean students to see how they

* So the command always sounded to me, though in full it
should be, " *Ki o tsuké* " (" Apply your minds ").

responded to this alien patriotism. To all
appearance they sang with much the same
abandon as the Japanese, though perhaps not
with the same ecstatic closing of the eyes, throw
back of the head, straining of the throat. And
certainly here and there a face or two showed
glum, remembering, possibly, the days when
Korea possessed an Emperor of her own. Yet
if so, they could have hardly wished him back.
He was an entirely ineffective old man, ruled by
a Chinese wife, whom the Japanese removed in
their own particular method when she obstructed
their policy. The Emperor, lost without her,
fled one morning in a woman's chair to the
Russian Embassy. Quite an effete Oriental
monarch who appeared occasionally among his
people, borne on a palanquin through streets
carefully cleared and cleaned for him, and lined
with soldiers. He would have yielded to the
persuasions of the missionaries, friends of his, and
become a Christian, promising to issue an edict
commanding the whole country to imitate his
conversion; but Christianity and concubines
appeared to be irreconcilable, and the concubines
won the day. His will was law, he flourished on
extortion, he lived in momently fear of assassina-
tion, he knew nothing of his people; his place
was in a museum, not on a throne. Surely the

Koreans had lost nothing in their forced submission to the strenuous Japanese cult. Yet the cult was Japanese.

The singing over, the Director ascended the platform, slowly, both feet halting on each step. From the table at the back he took a flat, black-lacquered box, bowed over it, bore it reverently, and placed it before him on the front table, bowed over it, loosened the securing ribbons, and removed the lid, bowed over it, folded back the corners of a silk wrapper and drew out a document, bowed over it, and holding it up before him commenced to read. It was the edict to the schools issued by the Emperor Meiji, exhorting to labour and obedience. Read in a sing-song of emphatic nasalities it sounded quite impressive. The reading completed, it was returned to its place with reversed ceremonial. Then followed the Director's harangue.

I could not understand a word. But the little fellow, customarily rather self-effacing and extremely polite, took on an amazing animation. The students watched him with undiverted eyes, with never a smile, expressionlessly intent. But they must have known exactly what he intended to say before he opened his lips. It was impossible that he should have deviated from his official creed of Loyalty and Piety. By virtue

of his place that was his only text, his only
sermon.

But I am doomed to a discordant memory
which robs these ceremonies of their solemnity.
On one occasion when we had bowed to the
portrait and were waiting for the curtains to
close over it, we found ourselves arrested with
bent backs because the curtains remained obsti-
nately apart. It was impossible to straighten
ourselves while the Presence was in view. The
Director, inclined in front of us, coughed
discreetly, coughed with authority. The curtains
remained apart. Then at last I discovered the
purpose of that cupboard. The teacher nearest
to it approached it, with hands on thighs and
back bent almost at right angles, an attitude
which gave him the appearance of minutely
scrutinizing the floor. He opened the door and
held a whispered consultation with some one
concealed within. Of course a school servant
whose duty it was at the appointed moment to
pull the cord. The teacher returned, in the
same attitude of scrutiny. We continued bowed,
glancing up at the curtains from under lowered
brows. Still they did not move. A hitch in the
mechanism of a piece of string threatened to hold
us in that hall all day in postures of profound
humility, awed by a portrait. The teacher

D

approached the cupboard a second time. Then
suddenly with a leap the curtains fell together.
The portrait veiled was no longer a thing of
power. We straightened in relief.

I cannot get that out of my mind; nor the
later adventures of that picture. For reasons
which I have already explained, it would have
been unwise to leave it in its alcove, a prey to
spiteful enemies and fire. A granite safe was
built for it—as was customary at all the schools—
set to one side of the drive and planted about
with trees; for all the world like a latrine. But
before the safe was built the picture was kept
for security in the porter's lodge. It was hung
on a wall opposite a window which overlooked
the road. But this was inconvenient, because
all passers-by were obliged to stop and bow.
It was changed to another wall. But this
time it was visible from the tennis courts, which
occasioned incongruous reverences when a
player's eyes chanced that way. There was
nowhere else to hang it, the lodge appearing to
consist of two walls and two windows. *Saa!*
What to do about it?

It was turned face to the wall.

As it arrived that day a cohort of waiting
policemen surrounded the car, while others kept

at bay suspicious prowlers. The resplendent drill major called " *Kirits !* " and we sprang to attention, called " *Rê !* " and we bowed.

It was carried up the drive between us, bowed so in a double row. A policeman preceded it, followed by the Director—in evening dress—who bore it before him, veiled, holding it at the full stretch of his arms with his head bent over it, himself followed by a further train of policemen. The procession moved with a slow deliberation, as though in fear lest the portrait should be shaken in its frame, causing sympathetic disquietudes to the Son of Heaven in his palace at Kyoto. And not till the school door closed safely behind it did the drill major call us back to rectitude.

We saw it later : a couple of half-crown photographs, I should say, the Emperor in marshal's uniform, the Empress in a Western robe and crown, framed together in a white wood frame.

Yet there was a fineness in its cheap simplicity. One would not inquire its price in dollars. And if it represented what it pretended to represent it was beyond price, a force incalculable.

We ate cuttlefish and drank *saké* in its honour. The cuttlefish was cut into hard, hairy strings.

It tasted faintly of salt as one chewed it, and was more endurable than gum. The *saké* we drank warm from minute bowls. Those who drank plentifully became merry. It is the Japanese national wine, of no particular virtue.

But please don't call it " sacky."

IV

INNS

IT was Yu See Kuk who introduced me to
my first Korean inn. I accompanied him
with a certain misgiving, for I had read
much and heard more ; details of night life, you
understand, which made one shudder. I believe
I was threatened, too, with typhoid and cholera
if I attempted to live on Korean food. The warning was well meant, though a trifle exaggerated.
And in any case I was already committed.

The fact was that I wished to visit Kyung Ju
(in Japanese pronunciation Keishu), an old
capital of an earlier dynasty where one might
see the best of Korean art. It seemed better
to travel with a native student who understood
the place than with a foreign missionary who
pretended to. Incidentally I lived in an atmosphere of foreign missionary, and it was pleasant
for a little to escape it. But travelling with a
native I was obliged to limit myself to his means.
A Japanese inn would have been beyond his
purse, quite apart from his rooted detestation of

all things Japanese. A Korean inn was the only alternative.

But I'm writing as though I consented to the alternative purely because it was unavoidable. This was not so at all. I was ext remely anxious to sample the native hostelry. Secretly I was hoping for a full portion of the reported horrors. And the amazing state of dirt of the ordinary Korean house, and the daily vision of squatting figures by doorways and gutters and street corners rolling back their clothing in a leisurely pursuit of lice, seemed to promise that I should not be disappointed. I imagined myself returning, stripping in the garden and making a bonfire of my clothing, and from there heading straight for the bath. Still, I wasn't exactly hankering for typhoid or cholera.

From the capital we took the night train south to Taiku. It was part of the financial condition that we should travel third class. You understand that it would have been impossible for me to offer to defray a single sen of my companion's expenses. Eastern pride could not have endured the affront, and I should have made an enemy for ever. I was prepared to sit up all night on a wooden bench in an atmosphere of smoke and garlic ; but no such thing. There were bunks arranged in a triple tier, upholstered, though thinly, with a hard pillow, but no bedding. It was the end of March, and the weather was still wintry, but the compartment was so well heated that if one did not undress one needed no bedding. In fact, the bunk was more comfortable than in a first- or second-class carriage where one lay on a soft mattress, beneath a pile of blankets, behind curtains, unable to sleep for stuffiness and heat. Here the air blew refreshingly down the length of the coach. It was no sort of preliminary to my anticipated discomforts. In fact, I was deciding that in future I should always travel this way. But the discomforts might await me yet.

We disembarked at Taiku at six in the morning. For two hours we must wait at the station before we could travel by the local motor service (Ford car) to Kyung Ju. But the Japanese provide warm waiting-rooms. We spent the time fitfully continuing our broken sleep, and in breakfast. Not quite knowing what lay ahead of me, I ordered " baconeggs " in the manner of a man feasting well before plunging into the wilds.

I think there were nine of us in that Ford car ; but the intimate contact of bodies kept us warm, which was comforting with the sharp air of the morning cutting like a knife through the gaps of the flapping wind-screens. The ride lasted two hours along an excellent road—by which one means merely that it was hard—built straight and high like a causeway above the muddy rice-fields, dipping suddenly to fords where it crossed the stony beds of streams. But at the end of the journey I found myself stiff and numb, and much colder than I had thought. Indeed, I was violently shivering. And the destination was cheerless. Kyung Ju, judging by its main street, seemed little more than a village. Between its lines of tiled-roofed, single-storied houses, with no sign of the West there, with hardly a sign of Japan, I felt something of the same sense of desolation as one felt in the war when taking up new billets in some lost and broken Flemish hamlet. While my companion made inquiries I stood idly by receiving no impressions except one of vague abandonment, and when, after an infinite discussion, which slowly sucked into it half the male inhabitants of the street, he seemed to have come to some conclusion I followed him tamely without a word.

We turned into a side street where a single cart could hardly have passed between the open sewers by the blank, mud walls. But at the end the street widened a little, and here we came upon our inn.

The enclosing walls, roofed with tiles, were

indeed of stone, but the entrance promised little cheer. A double gateway, inscribed down the sides with Chinese characters, opened between two tiny, papered windows like unseeing eyes. But once within the courtyard the place looked more prosperous, more hospitable. It was built four-square, with a block of guest-chambers to either side, and opposite us the host's rooms and the kitchen. A girl was drawing water from a well. A woman was crouched beside the kitchen fire stirring messes in round, flat, iron pans. At the sight of us entering they ceased their drawing and their stirring like mechanical figures whose clockwork had run out. They became two pairs of eyes expressionlessly at gaze. My companion took no notice of them. He advanced to the centre of the courtyard and, clapping his hands, called a summons, with a certain imperiousness of tone warrantable in a University student accompanied by a white man. And a University professor at that. From a low doorway opposite the host appeared with the startled suddenness of a rabbit smoked out of a hole. He was obliged to stoop to pass beneath the lintel. He stepped into a pair of canoe-shaped rubber shoes, which lay ready on the raised platform outside the door, came down from the platform, and advancing to within a few yards of us bowed, and muttered expressions of polite welcome.

It was some little while before we were duly installed. Of course we must have the best room. We passed into a second courtyard, something more sumptuous, bounded on three sides by guest-chambers, and on the fourth by the street wall. Having examined all the rooms and selected one, which was accordingly swept for us, set with cushions, cigarettes and ash-trays, and having removed our boots and settled ourselves cross-legged on the cushions, my companion chose to find some defect. Again clapping his hands, he called for the host, who had left us to see to fire and food, and announced that the room was not suitable. A fresh room was chosen, exactly similar, as far as I could see, to the one we had left, was swept for us, set with cushions, cigarettes and ash-trays, and we settled ourselves as before. But in a few minutes my companion was up again, passing backwards and forwards from the old room to the new. He thought, perhaps, the old room was the better. But I had no intention of moving a second time. I said that I greatly preferred the room we were in, it was much more convenient than the other, to which he smiled in instant agreement. I thought the occasion called for a pipe.

THE INN COURTYARD

The room was about nine feet square, one of
three in a block facing the street wall. The three
rooms opened into each other by sliding screens,
and on to a covered platform outside by papered
doors of fretted woodwork. Such light as there
was filtered through the opaque cream paper of
the door, shut now against the cold. There was
no furniture except a four-inch-high table and a
mirror in a swinging frame which stood on the
floor. The floor was laid with thick, oiled paper
securely glued down. Beneath, I knew, were
granite slabs, the interstices well plastered,
arranged over long flues ; for the Koreans heat
their houses in Roman fashion with fires from
beneath. On the floor were set the thin cushions
on which we squatted. It felt cold to our
stockinged feet, but gradually it grew warmer,
became hot, so that we were obliged to tuck our
feet on to the cushions, as the fire which our
host had lit for us made its presence felt. The air,
too, lost its penetrating chill. We opened the
door.

There was nothing to look at except the empty
courtyard bounded by the blank wall, and to
either side the flanking blocks, exact counterparts of our own, with their three little doors in a
row and covered platforms.

Food was brought to us. Presumably a second

breakfast. It was set on separate tables in dishes and bowls of brass, with brass chop-sticks and a flat brass spoon.   A boy was in attendance to serve us with rice, and our host settled himself in a corner, squatting on his heels in the manner of the Koreans, and, asking permission, drew out a slender bamboo pipe and enjoyed a three-whiff smoke. He was a solemn-faced, thin man, with drooping lips, high cheek-bones, and a straggling goatee beard whose every hair showed distinctly detached as though separately inserted by some artificial process. He maintained a continual flow of conversation, occasionally tapping out his pipe and refilling it with a minute ball of fine hair-like tobacco. But, though his manner suggested that he had come to entertain his guests while they dined, his eyes upon me made one suspect that it was curiosity that had drawn him to observe the foreigner. But he was too polite to betray any amusement at my clumsiness. Indeed, he was very polite. I learned later that he was of the Korean *yangban* (noble) class, abolished by the Japanese, and was now inn-keeping for a living.

I bent to my table. There was a thin soup, pungent with red pepper ; there were squares of bean curd ; there were poached eggs ; there were innumerable nameless dishes seasoned with

garlic and onion ; there were little pancakes,
and what seemed to me to be celery fried in
batter ; there were miniscular fishes which one
ate a dozen to the mouthful, highly savoury, and
spotted as they lay contorted together with
starting black shrimp's eyes ; and there was
kimchi, the native pickle, whose reek of sour
vinegar pervades the whole atmosphere of Korea ;
and there was rice. Plentiful rice, hot, white and
dry, with every grain distinct. And if one wished
to drink there was a shallow brass bowl of
brownish fluid, the water in which the rice had
been boiled.

I fed well. I found the fare appetizing, though
it was beyond me to eat more than a quarter of
what was provided. I began to wonder at the
stories I had heard of the inedibility of Korean
food. But I understood the stories better when
supper was an exact repetition of breakfast, and
the breakfasts and suppers that followed exact
repetitions of the breakfasts and suppers that
went before, with lunch between merely a
rehashing of what remained. I found myself
sickening with the fat, with the peculiar savours,
and hankered for plum cake and fruit. I could
have drunk quarts of tea ; I could have eaten
tins of biscuits. I had taken certain provisions
with me, but half-heartedly, in a reluctant

yielding to insistent advice. But among my
provisions there was nothing that tempted me,
except a tin of Kraft cheese. One day I opened
this, and found it delicious. I offered a piece
to Yu See Kuk. He nibbled a tiny end, and
promptly swallowed a bowlful of rice, for all his
Eastern politeness unable to repress violent
symptoms of sickness. Yet he would gorge on
that dreadful *kimchi.*

We spent the day among the temples and the
tombs.

It was little comfort to return in the evening
weary-limbed to find nothing more commodious
to rest on than a thin cushion on a hard floor.
And the floor was barely warm, as the fire had
burnt out.

To my amazement I learnt there was a bath.
A Japanese affair, I found it, installed in an
outhouse. It consisted of a deep iron cauldron,
the water heated by a fire from beneath. We
washed before entering, in approved fashion.
Chilling draughts blew in upon us from the ill-
fitting doors and windows, and in contrast the
water we poured over us was stinging hot. Yu
See Kuk ventured first into the cauldron, and
sprang out with a yell, holding to a scorched foot.
He was evidently unaccustomed to Japanese
baths. I was able to teach him something of the

East. The bath possessed a wooden lid. One
stood on this, forcing it to sink, till it wedged
itself against the side some inches from the
bottom, which, with the fire under it, was hot
enough to take the skin from one's feet.

After supper the bedding was brought in and
laid upon the floor. So far the place had
appeared to me scrupulously clean. There was
no opportunity for dirt to gather on the smooth,
oiled floor. I thought the promised horrors
might be concealed in the bedding. But the
bedding was a miracle of spotlessness : a couple
of silken quilts, white for the mattress, crimson
for the coverlet, but tacked across the top with a
white band. It was a shame to wear any night
gear. If I had been alone I should have rolled
myself between them naked. And now, with
the fire replenished, the floor was hot again, a
genial warmth penetrating from beneath lapped
one from head to foot in an instantaneous
beatitude. It would be difficult to rise in the
morning.

But we did rise, and washed outside on the
platform in basins of hot water which left the
skin shiveringly sensitive to the freezing air.
And in the corner of the courtyard was a latrine.
That at least was orthodox Korean. Yu See
Kuk cautioned me against it, beseechingly, as

though suggesting that for a few days I might abstain. If the rest of the inn had been in keeping with that latrine the dark prophesyings of my well-wishers would have been abundantly fulfilled, perhaps even to typhoid and cholera.

Our entertainment cost us two yen (four shillings) a day.

Yet there *are* such inns as my friends described to me. There was one across the road. We watched a play there, given by a company of strolling players, exactly in the manner of our own early drama. A peep into the tiny rooms —like rows of animals' cages—revealed to me all that I had escaped.

But here is the most unique description of a Korean inn that has ever been written, because, except negatively, it makes no mention of insect-powders and horrible creeping things.

And it is all quite true.

THE TEMPLE OF PUL KUK SA, NEAR KYUNG JU

V

KWAN-OK-SAN

SHE was a spinster, and her name was Turniptops. Or rather, to judge by her emphasis of the last syllable, it was probably hyphened : Turnip-Tops. Yet she was not ashamed to be making the round of the globe, inscribing that name in hotel registers, proclaiming it to strangers. Of course it was possible that she was seeking to alter it. I rather think the search will be in vain.

She arrived one evening at my hostess's house. She had already seen Japan and was on her way to China, allowing herself a single day to " do " Korea. She was not unique in this. It seems to have become an established custom among tourists of the Far East, a convention you might call it, to do Korea in a single day. Though once a party of Christian Young Men, who also boarded with my hostess, remained two days. But they were immature and irresponsible and with an undeveloped sense of the proportions of things. And once I met a lady who spent a

fortnight in the country.   But her soul must have
been rare and star-like.   And I believe she was
granted a vision ;   which would be upsetting
to the tourist, whose ambition appears to be
to tick off names in guide-books with the
maximum speed.

Miss Turniptops (or Turnip-Tops) had a pink
face and a hooked nose.   The outer edges of
her eyelids slanted down over her eyes, like
curtains looped back to either side of a double
window.   She was dressed in a frock of bunchy
and transparent muslin patterned with large,
faint flowers.   She sat upright on the sofa and
kept us out of bed till nearly midnight (my hosts
usually retired at nine), telling us all that she had
seen in Japan.

One or two of us had already been to Japan.

Also it was clear that she had not deviated an
inch from the prescribed routes.

She was intending to spend the next day in the
city, and leave by the night train.

" Only one day ? " I asked.

But my satire was lost on her.   Yes, only one
day, though she would have just loved, etc., etc.
And she drew out a copy of the Chosen Hotel
guide-book, and read to us a list of the places
she meant to visit : the Government House, the
North Palace, the East Palace, Independence

Arch, Pagoda Park. Read out like that the list sounded rather imposing; but having seen these things one was not impressed.

" While at the East Palace," I suggested to her, " you had better see the zoo."

She was instant attention, and rummaging in her hand-bag for a pencil sat with it poised, preparing to take notes.

" I suppose there are many rare specimens ? " she asked eagerly.

" It's quite unique," I told her. " There's a monkey-house ; and there are two elephants in a cage. You feed the monkeys with pea-nuts and the elephants with buns. It's awfully jolly."

I think from that moment she began to take a dislike to me.

Yet I did my best for her. I asked her to join a party, of which I was one, and come with us the next day (Sunday) to climb the Kwan-ok-san. I told her that the city would disappoint her, that the beauty of Korea was in its hills.

Of course she still thought I was teasing her. To spend her single day in the hills ! Besides, travelling up from the coast she had seen the hills. She had seen them from the train. As a sop to my possibly genuine good intentions she said that the hills were " just lovely." And that set her talking for another hour, while my host's head nodded and my hostess rocked herself violently in her chair, telling us all that she had seen of Korea from the window of her train.

We had also travelled in trains with windows.

The next morning—it was Sunday, you remember—my hostess thought it politic to inform Miss Turniptops (or Turnip-Tops) that I wrote books. This was to account for my unsabbatical costume. I was in shorts, tieless, my shirt collar folding over the collar of my tunic. Presumably this sort of thing was permissible in one who wrote books.

I wished Miss Turniptops a successful day, and shouldering my camera and rucksack set off for the station.

For a long time I had wanted to climb Kwan-ok-san. From the hills behind my house, ever since my first coming to Korea, I had looked across to it almost daily. It lay to the east across the river, a long serrated ridge rising to a fantastic central summit for all the world like a cock's comb. It bounded the view to that direction, a superb background to a wide sweep of ragged ranges. In shape it might have been some horny-backed monster of the primal swamps; in colour it glowed to the western sky a deep amber crested with violet. But this might be said of a thousand Korean mountains. Yet there was something peculiar in Kwan-ok-san. It came to me of a sudden one day that its peculiarity lay not in its strangeness but in its exact truth to type. Other hills had a quietude, a wildness, a suavity or a vigour, particular to themselves alone ; but Kwan-ok-san had that universal quality which arrests one occasionally in the poise of a tree, in the curve of a river, in a stormy sky, in a serene sunset, when one feels that if all other trees and rivers, all other storms and sunsets, were forgotten it would be sufficient to remember these. And it is so with me still. Kwan-ok-san remains in my mind as the perfection, the ideal. To conjure up the vision of this single mountain is to conjure up the whole of Korea.

Perhaps the essential appeal of the Korean mountains is that they cry to you to climb them. There is a strenuous challenge in them that will not let you rest. They are no mere pictorial settings for the valleys. They are pinnacles of outlook, and you are not satisfied till you have scaled each one to the topmost peak. That is, you are never satisfied, for the hills are legion ; a healthy spiritual state. The Koreans themselves are victims to this spell. Lazy and lethargic, slow-stepping and with eyes brimmed with sleep, even they cannot resist the call of their mountains. The older men will picnic on the summits, squatting on their heels to drink wine and smoke long pipes, and amusing themselves with dancing-girls and flute-players ; the younger men will leap among the rocks like goats, and plant themselves on dizzy crests and sing—also like goats. And Kwan-ok-san called like other mountains to which I had already yielded ; but more imperatively. It was good to know that the day for climbing it had come at last.

I met my friends at the station : several Germans, an American, an English girl, two Eurasian girls, some others. Not entirely respectable, perhaps. The Germans, for instance, had not yet been readmitted to the Club since their exclusion during the War. Many people still would not speak to them. The Eurasian girls, courted as dancing partners, were otherwise eyed askance. Yet I was at one with them all. Sunday by Sunday we made raids together into the hills. Ephemeral feuds, and the antipathies of blood and colour, were powerless against the everlasting rocks and the universal air.

A short train journey took us over the river to where the approach began.

We passed among rice-paddies, making towards the hills. Men in white, splashed to the shoulders, with pantaloons rolled up to the knees, and scarves about their heads, were ploughing in the last year's stubble. In the slow inconsequence of their movements they seemed as purely animal as the apathetic oxen that drew the ploughs, wading laboriously through the black ooze of the mud. Others were digging clear the irrigation ditches, three or five working to a single shovel, one holding the handle, the others heaving from in front at ropes attached to the blade. They worked without zeal, without speed, piling the mud up on the banks. *Jigi*-men passed us bearing enormous loads on their backs of fish and vegetables. By wayside runnels women squatted at their washing, everlastingly beating at the soiled white cottons with wooden clubs. A world of toil, of unquestioning patience, of unconscious content.

We reached the lower slopes. A narrow earth track, curving upwards, shelving by rounded bluffs of loose granite sand, and twisting between gaps and saddles, brought us to a temple. It was built on a platform of rock on the top of an immense boulder which thrust up out of the earth. Twisted pines clung to the crevices with a network of naked roots. We rested beneath the rock where a spring bubbled. A hollow for the water had been hewn in the granite and a channel cut for it to flow free. A long-handled dipper lay by the hollow. The water was crystal-clear and ice-cold, infinitely refreshing. Because already the morning was hot. It was early summer. The sky was of a deep blue unflecked by cloud, the sun growing powerful. A faint haze still lay about the horizon, but this was thinning. It was real Korean weather, beneficent and serene.

Suddenly from the temple above us drums boomed, and droning voices began lingeringly to intone an invocation to Buddha :

" *Naaa-mooo Aaa-meeda Booool !   Naaa-mooo Aaa-meeda Booool !* "

That would endure for hours.

Climbing up to the temple platform we could see the chanting priests in the shadow of the hall, cross-legged upon the paper-laid floor, their drums before them, their faces drawn in pained abstraction, oblivious as children of the surrounding world. And opposite the open door Buddha squatted behind the altar, backed by a medley of painted saints, gazing through a haze of incense smoke flushed with candle-light, but with eyes entirely expressionless and incapable of vision. There seemed no single correlation between this somnolent worship and the vigorous hills around.

Leaving the temple the slopes became steeper, the path dwindled out. We pushed among

shrubby pine, planted by the Japanese, and from
a crest took bearings for Kwan-ok-san looming
up from the valley below. The cock's-comb
summit showed now in its true aspect of stark
rocks. Deep gorges cut down from it to the
valley, green against the purple granite and the
yellow disintegrated sand. We singled out the
gorge which promised the readiest ascent, and
plunged for the valley through a world grown
suddenly wild. We lowered ourselves by rocks
and trees, clinging to roots, pushing through
entangling clumps of acacia. Striking a gully,
where water trickled and disappeared and oozed
out again between shrubs and boulders, we
followed it recklessly to find ourselves shut in to
either side with rocky walls which hid from us our
goal. There were only three of us now. Our
party had become divided. We halloed to each
other from time to time so as to keep in touch.
The trickling water became a slender torrent.
We could not cross it and recross at pleasure.
Choosing the bank which kept us nearer to
our friends we held to it, and after an hour of
hopping and leaping reached the valley below.

But the rest of our party, descending by another
gully, had aimed better than we, coming out
at the mouth of the gorge which led up the
mountain. To rejoin them we could have made

quite easily up the valley, but we preferred to cut
at a slant over the lower slopes of the mountain.
It was a foolish thing to do. We found ourselves
ankle-deep in loose sand on bluffs so steep that
we could scarcely maintain our balance. We
found ourselves in wildernesses of rocks and
pines. We were obliged to scale ridges and drop
into gullies, fatiguing ourselves unnecessarily
with an unceasing up-and-down progress. And
the sun was hot, and the air was dry. But we
came upon runnels where we could drink. And
it was splendidly exhilarating.

We struck the gorge at length. There were
still two hours before us of upward struggle.
We found our friends at the top seated at ease
among the stark boulders. They welcomed us
with an ironic superiority, mockingly incredulous
at our assertions that if the mountain were to be
climbed again we would choose the same route.

We lunched, smoked, lazed ; some of us slept.

There was still a higher peak to climb where
a temple was built on the edge of a precipice.
We made up to it by a track worn on the rock by
the rubbing of many feet. It led along the top
of a bare ridge, and dropped by a natural stair-
way in a cleft between boulders to a narrow
platform, so narrow indeed that one hesitated
to descend. But one descended. And rounding

a hump of rock came to the temple. It was a tiny building, red-pillared, backed against the cliff, and with a platform before it, perhaps a couple of yards wide, overlooking a sheer abyss.

But from here one had the pageant of the mountains full in view. Range beyond range of fantastic crests, wildly indented, seeming to curl over like waves, as though the whole land had been suddenly petrified in the midst of a molten agitation. Here, in spite of the temple behind, if one had worshipped it would not have been the impassive Buddha, but the Spirit of the Ancient Earth, cruel and adorable, of which Man is the creature.

We returned by another route. Men and boys scraped among the pines for fuel, twigs and leaves and needles. They used long, fan-shaped rakes, and gathering their fuel into bundles they bound them about with straw ropes, and piling them on to wooden frames set their backs to them, crouching low and steadying themselves laboriously to their feet by the aid of stout staves. And reaching the valleys we came again to the ploughing men and the washing women. Earth, earth, and earth ! With our eyes full of the hills this people took on a new significance. They might have risen from the soil, the harvest of some ancient dragon's teeth ; a dragon not of the rocks, but some wallowing monster of the mud. Yet the mountains were all about them, and at times they seemed to understand the mountains. At times. And perhaps only a few. For these were not the breed who leapt among rocks, and amused themselves with dancing-girls and flute-players. Those were the young, or the fortunate and liberated souls not constrained to grub ever-lastingly in the soil for a pitiable living.

The earth is not yet inherited of her children.

A last look at Kwan-ok-san, amber and violet with the sunset upon it, as the train carried us back across the river.

And this was how Miss Turniptops (or Turnip-Tops) must have seen it, from the window of her train. I was in time to meet her again. She had half an hour to spare before starting for the station, before leaving Korea for ever, having spent a whole day, " a perfectly lovely day," in the capital. She was telling my hosts of all she had seen : the Government House, the North Palace, the East Palace.

" Did you remember the zoo ? " I asked.

Certainly the earth is not yet inherited of her children.

THE WASHING WOMEN

VI

THE UNTYPICAL ENGLISHMAN

ONE met very few Englishmen in Korea, and as those few failed to conform to type I can't draw for you the customary caricature. There was one who would listen for three hours on end to gramophone records of classical music, and enjoyed it. There was another who spoke French with a perfect accent. Another was suspected of secret hankerings towards suicide. Another was a completely unmannered boor. You see my difficulty.

There was yet another whom I am singling out to describe.

Quite apart from his being thoroughly worth an introduction he throws a light on the motives which draw men abroad. Judging by the people one meets, out East at any rate, it is seldom romance which is the lure. The business man is hard, canny, brutal. Sometimes he is a gentleman ; but even so his object is money, and his ambition an early and comfortable retirement—at home. The Government official pursues promotion with an undeviating disregard of locality. The doctor is less intrigued by interesting diseases than by his phenomenal pay. The missionary, victim of a superiority complex and a sublimated *Wanderlust*, approaches nearer to the romantic ; but he is unaware of it, and he is speedily cured. This man, however, came East neither through an itching palm nor itching feet. He wanted to be alone.

A teaching appointment gave him his opportunity.

By the way, this is not myself that I am portraying in a subtly veiled parable. This man existed ; he exists. I shall have to apologize to him for exposing him in this way. Because his soul is somewhat owl-like, hating the light. And when I apologize he will look at me with a searching seriousness and say, " You don't mean it." Which, of course, will be true.

The mention of truth brings me at once to the secret of his loneliness. He found himself obliged by some sensitive compunction always to speak the truth. Which is unsociable. I have heard him, not once only, interrupt his wife in some amusing anecdote with a curt, " That's a lie." At which the dear lady, imaginatively garrulous, with a rather damp face and untidy hair, would break into a voluble justification. Not of the exactitude of her remark, but of the permissibility, indeed the necessity and the duty, of untruthfulness in conversation. For conversation to her was an art, not a dull interchange of information. And I'm afraid, from the latter point of view, she was an unscrupulous liar of the first order. When I became more familiar with the couple I was able to tell her so, with the frank directness of her husband. But it never perturbed her in the least. " Of course, if you only want dry facts . . . " Yet for the man, with his Puritanic conception of truth complicated by his wife's theory of conversation as an art, social intercourse was impossible. It was awkward to feel yourself obliged to tell people precisely what you thought of them, punctuating your remarks with abrupt announcements across the drawing-room that your wife was telling a lie. The only alternative was solitude.

Curiously enough people thought he was rude. He fled East, thinking that there he could bury himself among strangers whose language he would not understand, and whom, consequently, he would not be compelled to shock by his unfortunate virtue. His wife accompanied him, plucky lady. They lived at first in a Japanese inn, later in a Japanese house, sitting on cushions on the mat-laid floor and eating rice and raw fish

and seaweed. I believe they both fell ill. I
found them installed in a house of their own
building, well outside the east gate of the city.
One turned from the terminus of a single-line
tram route by a path that crossed among rice-
paddies and a brick-kiln and a village, up a slope
between humped graves, and came upon it set
high on a knoll. I was obliged to remove my
boots in a little Japanese vestibule before entering
by papered screens. But inside, on the ground
floor at least, the house was furnished in Western
fashion, though upstairs the rooms were set with
yellow Japanese mats. Also the sitting-room had
Western windows on one side and Japanese
windows on the other, opening on to a Japanese
veranda. It was warmed in winter by an
immense iron stove, which stood central in the
room, with a zinc pipe passing under the ceiling
and through a wall. There was a couch and
chairs, a small table, a carpet on a polished board
floor, and a grand piano. The pictures were
mostly Eastern, both Japanese and Korean.
Old Korean vases stood here and there, crude and
handsome ; and there were two Korean chests.
The lady took me the round of the vases and
the pictures, expatiating on their age, their
significance. I discovered that she had absorbed
an amazing amount of information during her

few years in the country, but later, when I knew her better, I wondered how much was fact and how much fable.

These people were vegetarians. The husband on principle, the wife, possibly on principle, possibly from necessity. I was served with continuous courses of apples and hard Japanese pears and bananas and slices of pineapple and bread and butter, provided at long intervals by a Korean woman, dressed in white, with clumsy fingers and a melancholy face.

I visited frequently. There must have been something peculiar about me, because I was sincerely welcomed ; a unique privilege, I soon discovered, when talking to other folk about the couple. People deplored their solitude, tried to break in upon it, making special journeys in a slow tram crowded with Koreans smelling of *kimchi* pickles, buzzing with flies, choking with dust, to be turned away at the door because no one was at home, or to be admitted after duly removing their shoes. The wife occasionally visited me ; but in visible agitation lest any of her well-wishers should come upon her in the streets and engage her for a tea-party. She was dreadfully timid of such invitations. Particularly she was terrified of a certain missionary lady who lived next door to me. She would make a long

F

detour through narrow twisting alleys between native hovels, up a steep hill, and down through the graveyard above the house I lived in, to avoid being seen by the missionary lady through her window which spied upon the main path. But there was a reason. The missionary lady, after a tea-party, had once persuaded her for the good of her soul to kneel down among the cake-stands and pray.

The man was a poet ; his wife was his single adorer. It was reported to me once—as an example of his madness or his rudeness or his unsociability, I'm not sure which—that once when he was asked why he didn't join more in the life of the community he answered, " I can't see people and write poetry too." It was his wife who gave me some of his poems to read— published in the *London Mercury*—while he sat severely by, squatting on a chair cross-legged like a Buddha hugging naked feet. To tell the truth I couldn't understand the poems very well. It was an awkward moment, which I delayed as long as possible, when the time came to express an opinion. I was torn between those rival theories of truth. But it doesn't matter very much what I said. At least I didn't forfeit their friendship.

But he was really a poet, in his attitude to life,

even in his appearance. He had a face of astonishing beauty, hazel eyes, long, brown, curling hair. It was unfortunate that he didn't shave more frequently, nor wash more scrupulously, nor take the trouble to brush away the accumulated scurf from the shoulders of his coat. It was difficult to penetrate beyond these things to the really startling beauty of his face. He worshipped Perfection. His wife played the piano, and had brought a grand with her from England ; but I could never persuade her to " favour me with a tune " because Reggie—from the beginning she referred to her husband by his Christian name—couldn't endure to listen to music which wasn't perfect. Instead they treated me to an occasional gramophone record, not permitting me to select what I preferred, but choosing something " perfect " which would be good for me to hear.

They slept on quilts on the floor.

The wife once asked me whether I went to church. She wasn't trying to convert me. Rather she was hoping to find in me an ally in her own non-attendance. Because the missionaries were continually laying siege to her ; but she put them off by telling the Presbyterians that she was a Methodist, and the Methodists that she was a Seventh Day Adventist, and

the Seventh Day Adventists that she was an
Episcopalian, always laying herself open to fresh
assaults.

"And what are you?" she suddenly asked
me.

I hedged.

" My parents are Baptists," I told her.

She burst into a wail of unconsolable self-
reproaches. How stupid she had been! She
hadn't thought of Baptists. That would have
ended the whole matter, because there were no
Baptists in Korea.

Yet she might have ended the matter quite
simply by telling the truth. She was a Jewess by
birth. But presumably she had schooled herself
so completely to falsehood that the truth never
obtruded itself upon her even when it would have
served her purpose.

The setting of the solitary house was romantic
in the extreme. Beyond the surrounding rice-
paddies the hills rose up abruptly to sharp, hard
crests. Green gullies striped the steep slopes
between bluffs of grey granite and humps of
tawny sand. We strolled together along the
tops of low ridges. My friend would say to me,
" There's a Buddhist temple on that mountain,"
or " That hill is always blue." And behind his
precise information I felt a passion for beauty too

sensitive to express itself in common words. It was quite unnecessary that his wife should break in with an explanatory gush, " Reggie loves that hill. I think he would die if you took away that hill." I wanted to promise not to take it away, but frivolity sank rebuked before the fixed regard of those hazel eyes. I wondered whether I was in the presence of another Shelley.

Once I provoked a discussion on vegetarianism. I knew immediately that I had committed an unpardonable offence, like violating a hospitality, or desecrating a shrine. The discussion soon resolved itself into an impassioned defence of Reggie by his wife. She became really heated, I believe a little hysterical, while her husband sat by silent and austere. I gathered that he ate no meat because of his shrinking from taking life.

" Reggie loves animals," his wife battered at what must have seemed to her my intentional scepticism, though I was prepared to believe that on this occasion she was speaking the truth. " It's impossible to tell you how he loves animals. It's one of those things you can't explain to people because they're too gross to understand. He loves animals better than anyone who has ever lived," she declared in a final assault upon my incredulity, adding, " except St. Francis of Assisi."

And it must have been so, because her husband did not contradict her. There was no sign of annoyance, no sign of amusement, in his grave regard. He accepted the statement without qualification, acknowledging it by his silence to be the exact truth. When he did speak it was to say :

" I used to be a Christian, but when I became a vegetarian I ceased to be a Christian because Christ ate meat."

When I first visited him he owned two dogs, large animals, their coats patchy with white and brown, with blood-shot eyes and pendent ears. A month later there were four dogs, later still six, eight. He couldn't kill them. He couldn't give them to the Koreans because they would eat them. They were a multiplying problem. He also kept chickens. When they ceased laying he continued to keep them. They had done their life's work, he told me, and deserved to be pensioned off like other people. He kept horses, goats. I forget how many goats. He kept monkeys. The male was no celibate ; the female quite obviously had reached the age of consent. Indeed, they paraded their incontinence in the manner of their species. But they had no issue. That was a pity, because I wanted to see how the problem of a growing

WINTER

family of monkeys would have been solved on the principle of take no life.

Yet there are limits. My friends came to England this year on a short visit. Not to see their people, I am convinced, but because it necessitated a clearance of the increasing menagerie. The dogs were given to the Koreans, the monkeys to the zoo. My friends have now returned to Korea. I presume they can make a fresh start with empty kennels and cleaned cages. It would be a favourable opportunity to call upon them before they have time to breed a new colony of dogs. Because those dogs were dangerous. They ranged the countryside, and met you a mile from the house, pursuing you with fierce barkings, and rushing in upon you when you turned your head, so that your final approach was a slow backing up the path with swinging stick. Once they tore my trousers. I suppose it was some consolation to be told, quite truthfully, that it was lucky I was wearing an old suit.

And there are other limits. During our discussion I asked :

" How about mosquitoes ? "

That problem was partly obviated by the doors and windows being screened. The nearest answer I got was when my friend rose, swotter in hand, and pursued a buzzing fly.

" If it is necessary to kill," he told me with a sad seriousness, " one must do so without the joy of the hunter." And in the manner of a man performing a distasteful duty he solemnly swotted the fly.

When my wife joined me in Korea we received an invitation to tea. We arrived at the appointed time, fighting our way through the barking dogs. The native woman of clumsy fingers and melan-choly face admitted us rather dubiously. We removed our boots and entered the sitting-room. But no one was at home to receive us. Perhaps a quarter of an hour later the husband appeared, in a villainous old suit, grimed from head to toe, his feet naked, his face unshaved, his long hair in wild disorder. He had been gardening, he had been grooming his horse. Would we excuse him, he must have a bath. Another half-hour passed, and the wife appeared. She was hot and moist and apologetic. She had suddenly remembered that we were coming to tea so had had to rush away to the city to buy some cakes. She explained this many times while she disposed parcels about the room. After a further wait tea was served, as I have already described it to you, in courses of fruit at long intervals. Then an argument began to develop between our hostess and the waiting woman. Our hostess rose and began to examine her parcels, went into the kitchen, returned and re-examined her parcels, then turned suddenly upon her husband with a plaintive :

" Oh, Reggie, where have you hidden those cakes ? "

She had left them in the tram.

But she was only convinced of it after repeated denials from Reggie and relentless searchings of the room.   She nearly wept.

" And we never have cakes," Reggie said ruefully, " except when visitors come."

But his wife was considering the disaster from another point of view.   " Never mind "—she turned to us with a sudden consolation—" I will post them to you."

The Japanese and the Koreans found my friend a little incomprehensible.   They thought of Englishmen as lords, living in society, elegantly dressed and with refined manners.

" But he live all alone," they said.   " Surely that not English custom.   Also very dirty, so I think.   We see him kiss monkey.   Is that English custom to kiss monkey ? "

" Well, you see," I answered, not wishing to betray either my friend or my countrymen, " he's a poet.   He isn't typical."

" Of course," they tittered, having presumably some dim idea that I had made a joke, " he not typical."

I intended to convey the impression of something rather fine and unique.   But I seem to have failed somehow.   It certainly looks as though I shall have to apologize.

VII

KEIJO

IF you look at a map of Korea, unless it is a
very recent one, you will find that the
capital is named Seoul. This is the Korean
name, and seems to be pronounced varyingly
as Seyool, Sowl, Sool, Sole. But the Japanese
have renamed the city Keijo.

The older residents naturally use the Korean
name as they have grown accustomed to it.
The missionaries also, but for the added reason
that they find a very human satisfaction in
annoying the Japanese. Their deliberate use of
" Seoul " appears to me much like the White
Russians' deliberate use of " St. Petersburg " :
a refusal to recognize a new and unwelcome order
of things. But, whether it really annoys the
Japanese, I don't know.

You may wonder why the Japanese should
change the name. As a matter of fact it is a
change in pronunciation merely, not in essence.
It is due to the use of Chinese characters by
both the Japanese and Koreans. The written

name remains unaltered. It simply happens that the two characters used are pronounced in one language as Keijo and in the other as Seoul. This applies to all towns in Korea, even to the name of Korea itself, though here the difference is slight : Chosen for Chosun. Usually the difference is more marked than this : Wonsan becomes Gensan ; Kyungju becomes Keishu ; and Chemulpo, the port of Keijo, becomes quite unrecognizable as Jinsen. You see, it is a little confusing, because you must learn a double list of names.

This applies also to the people. When a Korean boy goes to school he is addressed in the Japanese equivalent of his name, just as an English boy named William attending a French school would be addressed as Guillaume. Sometimes I found this disconcerting. A student whose name, for instance, was printed in the register as Hyo Bun Kyo would sign himself on his exercises as Pyo Moon Hoo ; and for the most part I only knew the Korean students by their Japanese names. Which probably rankled in their hearts, making them consider me an enemy to their country. At any rate, those who visited me were always careful to let me know, more or less pointedly, the correct pronunciation of their names.

But I am really meant to be telling you something of the capital.

Its situation is picturesque in the extreme. It lies in a hollow of granite hills within the elbow of a river. The city proper is withdrawn from the river some two miles, but to the south the hills open in a wide gap through which the city has overflowed to the river bank.

Its relation to the rest of the country is best expressed by saying that it lies midway on the railway that links Japan with Manchuria, being a twelve hours' train journey both from the northern frontier town of Antung and the southern port of Fusan. Its own port, Jinsen (Chemulpo), lies some twenty-five miles to the west ; and to the east it is connected with the port of Gensan, and by a line continuing north along the coast with the north-eastern frontier, terminating a little inland at the town of Kwainei. The railway system is best visualized as an inverted letter A, in this manner :

Antung   Kwainei

Keijo   Gensan

Fusan

But Kwainei is considerably farther north than Antung, and the Gensan-Fusan line, though under construction, is not yet finished. A further port is to be built somewhere to the north-east, and the line continued beyond Kwainei across Manchuria. When this has been completed Japan will be in absolute control of the Manchurian export trade. And central in this system of commercially strategic railways is the capital.

Tastes differ so, that if you paid a visit to Keijo I'm not sure what you would be interested to see. Possibly the silk and tobacco factories. Yet they are like others of their kind, except that hours are longer and pay less than in Europe— twelve hours a day for seven days a week, for ten to twenty yen (twenty to forty shillings) a month. But for the rest, they have tall brick chimneys, and they hoot the hands to work in the morning exactly as in the West. The Government building is more attractive, handsomely constructed in granite and with a central dome, approached by a wide, straight road so that its really excellent proportions can be appreciated without straining the neck. Within, it is cool and spacious, the central hall floored and columned with beautiful marble quarried in the country. And it is well situated. Behind it rises the toothed ridge of the northern mountains, setting it in white relief against a wild, dark

GOVERNMENT HOUSE, KEIJO

background. But there is more in its situation
than this picturesqueness of contrast. The spot
has been most exactly chosen to emphasize a
contrast more sinister. That solid and resolute
white building, lying like a barrier across the
wide, straight road, shuts away behind it the
principal imperial palace of Korea. Shuts it
away with a deliberate effacement. This is no
mere chance symbol. Its significance is intended.
And it is not only the present shutting away the
past—that is universal, and inevitable—it is
Japan shutting away Korea.

Another example of the unpardonable ill-
taste of the dominant nation. It is necessary
that Japan should shut many doors, but it is not
necessary that she should slam them with a
calculated provocation in one's face.

If you climb those northern hills—and you
will enjoy the climb—you can look down upon
the old palace grounds. Here and there the
outer walls, crumbling now and falling, can be
traced wandering inconsequentially among the
magnificent pines. You can see bridges and
gateways and a winding stream, the lake with
the summer pavilion lying out upon it as though
afloat, and standing up somewhat more loftily
the throne room, in a rectangular enclosed
courtyard, the broad sweep of its ribbed roof

uplifted at the corners, giving it the appearance
of an enormous tent. All this in itself is not
very impressive, being an inferior imitation of
the palaces of China. And one knows that it
was a centre of ineffective misgovernment and
puerile corruption. Yet walled blindly in from
all view of the city by that symbol of a foreign
but efficient administration, there is a pathos in
it, a suggestion. For it is not simply that one
finds oneself asking, " By what right does Japan
rule in Korea ? " The doubt penetrates more
deeply : " By what law are the weak devoured of
the strong ? " It is not a human law, for human
justice and human pity rebel against it. But it
is too powerful for human justice and human
pity, because too fundamental. The world is
driven along the path of its destiny by forces
imperative and ruthless. " It is the gods, the
gods above, that govern our condition. . . ."

Parts of the grounds are open to you. You
may rest, for instance, in the summer pavilion,
seeming to float upon the water in an enormous
barge, shaded from the heat by an immense
canopy slenderly columned. But you are not
admitted to the throne room. Yet once I found
myself there with two friends of mine, as one of
the gates of the enclosing wall had been left
unlocked. It was an exact replica, except for its

THE SUMMER PAVILION, THE IMPERIAL PALACE, KEIJO

size, of other rooms in other palaces, an exact
replica, for that matter, of temple halls and
chambers in rich men's homes. Built something
to one end of the paved courtyard, it stood on a
granite base approached by granite steps, with
the same grey tiled roof, the same dull red cedar
columns, the same walls and doors of fretted
wood papered from within, the same elaborately
decorative eaves gaudy with the same intricate
designs and bright colours which are universal
in the more sumptuous buildings of Korea.
The East is repetitive and monotonous. But
inside was the old throne : a rather uncomfortable double chair of wood set on a dais and
surmounted by a dragon canopy. In the dim
and empty interior it showed forlorn and faded.
It was difficult to imagine it the scene of a
vanished splendour.

It was very dim in the interior, because the
door swung to behind us with a clang, locking
us in. I can't tell you how long we struggled
at that lock. And we were afraid to shout
because we were on forbidden ground. There
was no knowing how the Japanese authorities
would have interpreted our trespass. You see,
we had cameras with us. One of my companions,
a Father of the English Church, dressed in a
long, black cassock and with a crucifix at his

breast, kept repeating, " Really, you know, this is most distressing. . . ."

If you wish to avoid a similar mishap you may see quite enough to satisfy you in the East Palace. This is now a public recreation ground, with zoo attached, and restaurants, and a lake where you can skate daily for two months of the winter. There is also an avenue of cherry-trees, planted by the Japanese, a magnificent sight towards the end of April, especially when illuminated at night ; and seasonal displays of peonies and chrysanthemums. But even if you cannot time your visit for any of these, there are other more serious interests. The halls and pavilions, of similar design to the throne room, are spaced in pleasant isolation among the trees. For the Korean fashion is not to set up a single immense block of buildings in the centre of a park, but to disperse the chambers so as to cover the whole ground. The suggestion is one of leisurely charm, of commodious ease. But these chambers now are used as a museum, to house such scanty treasures of pottery, painting and sculpture as Korea possesses. Also you can obtain permission to visit the summer gardens, enclosed behind the public grounds. Here you will see other halls and courtyards, more dreamlike, more dainty, and brooklets and lakelets and

THE THRONE ROOM, THE IMPERIAL PALACE, KEIJO

winding paths, where the Emperor amused
himself with his concubines in a manner befitting
the despot of an oppressed and impoverished
land.

Keijo once possessed a city wall. The northern
half of it still remains, though in varying stages
of decay. It was not built four-square like the
wall of Peking, but on the principle of a child's
afternoon scramble. You can see it suddenly
running up to the very tops of the pinnacled
hills, pausing a moment, as it were, to look
round and recover breath, then plunging for the
valleys in a wild glissade down precipitous slopes.
And the top, shaped in steps, gives it the
appearance of holding itself erect, mounting on
its toes, descending on its heels. Here and there
the archers' loop-holes are still intact, slanting
downwards ; but one fails entirely to trace the
strategic plan of its construction. It winds
and doubles upon itself in a manner seriously
to increase its length, and embraces so wide a
sweep of mountain far outside the last houses of
the city, that one wonders how it could ever have
been manned. But to follow its caprices is an
interesting Sunday occupation, and from its
higher vantages one can see the city in a wide
perspective impossible from the streets.

Speaking roughly, the city is quartered by two

great thoroughfares, running from north to south and from east to west. There are others, amply proportioned, parallel to these. Three main roads open out into the country : south across the river, east, and north-west through a gap in the hills—called the Peking Pass—to Chemulpo and the sea. This gap is called the Peking Pass because it was by this road that the Chinese envoys used to come, in the days of China's suzerainty, to collect tribute from Korea. The King—he was only a king then—used to meet them at a point outside the West Gate. Now at that point there is a stone arch, called Independence Arch, built when the Japanese liberated Korea from the overlordship of China. It was then that the King became an Emperor, which in the East means the monarch of an independent state. But Independence Arch will hardly tempt you to waste a film. It is a shabby little affair, already showing ominous cracks. And it does not even span the road, but stands to one side as though pushed there in deliberate and contemptuous neglect. A fit symbol of Korean independence.

The hills that bound the city on the west drop in lessening humps towards the river—they are a favoured locality for the foreign residents, whose houses you can see there standing red-bricked

and conspicuous in a lordly dominance of the
hovels below—but on the east the hills fail for a
space, to rise again between the East Gate and
the South Gate to a solitary cone, the Nam San.
One picnics there quite frequently, dreaming
away the splendid afternoon among twisted
pines and granite boulders. On the slope that
overlooks the city the Japanese have built a
Shinto shrine. It is approached by a magnificent, wide staircase of granite, between granite
lanterns and granite *torii* gates, and stands on a
natural platform beneath a rocky and precariously timbered cliff. A level road, lined with
hanging lanterns, curves away around the hill,
giving by frequent steep descents on to the main
Japanese quarter of the city. But if you climb
upwards in an attempt to reach the summit you
will find your way barred by barbed wire. If,
however, you persist, you will come upon further
remains of the old wall on the very peak. But
actually to climb to the peak is forbidden, as the
barbed wire suggests, because from here you
look down upon the Shinto shrine, an insult to
the gods. Yet the peak has an interest of its
own. It was here that in the old days a beacon
lay ready for kindling—the climax of a series
that encircled the country—to warn the Emperor
in his palace of coming danger. Not, presumably,

that he might summon his army to meet it, but that he might summon his personal retainers to carry him to safety in one of his mountain retreats. But there is no beacon on Nam San now ; and even to stand upon the spot is an offence because of that shrine of an alien worship which has usurped the slope below.

Yet Keijo is not merely a tilting ground for Japan and Korea, with Japan inevitably victorious. It is a tilting ground for East and West, with the West not so inevitably victorious because robbed of its conquest by parody and distortion. You will look in a shop window and see two Koreans sitting on the floor with a Singer sewing-machine between them, one turning the handle and the other manipulating the cloth. You will see a Japanese in frock coat and bowler hat, but with naked feet shod in flat, wooden clogs. And you will see brick houses and trams and cars, and you will hear music played on pianos and violins. But the houses are built at all angles ; in the trams the passengers deposit their packages on the seats and themselves remain standing ; the cars, intended to accommodate four or five, are provided with an extra bench to accommodate three more, so that you must climb over the back wheel to enter, tie your luggage on to the footboards and the radiator, and submit to an unrelenting and excruciating cramp ; and the noises that issue from the pianos and the violins are so perseveringly discordant that one is obliged to impute to the performers some hideous malevolence towards all mankind. But it is sufficient merely to see these people in Western clothes. They know neither how to make nor how to wear them. The trousers, except that they open in front—quite obviously !—might by their shape be reversible. They divide a full six inches too low. They are of the American pattern—that is, supported by a belt instead of braces ; but the Easterner has no hips, and the belt is certain to miss a loop or two, so when the jacket is off, which is frequent, the trousers hang from the waist in uncertain festoons overlapped by tags of shirt. Boots may or may not be worn ; but, in any case, as the Korean must remove his boots before entering his house it is more convenient to wear them without laces. In summer it is cooler to discard the outer garments altogether and dress in vest and pants alone. Fly buttons appear to be worn as ornaments.

All this would not vastly matter if it were merely an affair of sartorial incongruity. But one cannot avoid the implication in it of a fundamental attitude, a vital misconception.

For the East wears our thoughts as it wears our clothes.

So it is best to escape to the native quarters where the people can live their own lives in their own manner. That is, to escape from Keijo to Seoul. But that will need another chapter.

VIII

THE PEKING PASS

NOT long since, I received from the Poetess a delicately bound volume of delicate verse.* The themes are mostly of Japan, which the Poetess knew and loved ; but a few are of Korea, which she is learning to know and love. Their atmosphere is one of wistful enchantment ; they set you listening as though for echoes. In writing to express my thanks I said, intending the highest of compliments, that they were reading for the evening, before a blazing fire, with a pipe on. And among them is one entitled " The Road to Peking." I have it before me now. This is how it begins :

Between the hills it winds away—the high road to Peking.
The bullock carts go down it in a long, unbroken string ;
The rickshas and the buses, a shabby palanquin,
An old man like a drowsy god nods wearily within,
Dreaming of days when men were proud to own a
    palanquin.
Now motor-cars sweep by him and cover him with dust ;

---

* " Lanterns by the Lake," by Joan S. Grigsby.   Kegan Paul, Trench, Trübner & Co., Ltd., London.

His gold-embroidered curtains are soiled with moth and rust,
And no one asks his bearers who the rich man is they bring
Through crowds that throng at twilight the highway to
    Peking ;
For no one cares that once he was a courier to a king.

This suggests to me that I might recommend you to pay a visit to the road of the Peking Pass. You may see a great deal of Seoul here without burrowing too intimately among the alleys. If you are a poet like my friend the street may fill for you with the splendour of old pageantries, and a gentle melancholy will invade you brooding on departed things. But I cannot work that spell for you. On the hill-tops I had my visions too ; but in the streets the actual made too close a contact. I had eyes only for the visible, ears only for the audible, and a nose . . . I could willingly have dispensed with a nose. . . .

However, as an introduction to Seoul, I cannot advise you better than to take a leisurely stroll the length of the Peking Pass.

Imagine it a wide street, unpaved—except on occasions when cart-loads of loose shingle are emptied upon it to be swiftly absorbed at the first rain—flanked to either side by low, tiled-roofed, open-fronted shops, paraded by unhasting white figures, surmounted by a serene blue sky. A picture in slow motion, drab in colour except on days of festival, yet dazzling with the glare of glossy white robes in the relentless sunshine. And at every yard something to arrest you, to amuse you, possibly to shock you, to set you speculating, and if you have the photographic itch, to keep your camera in a continuous clicking.

You will soon recognize the most distinctive features. Oxen, single or in file, are bringing fuel in from the hills, or are drawn up by the road-side where they will stand all day till the fuel is sold. They are stacked high with bundles of pine branches, acacia branches, scrapings of twigs and leaves and needles bound about with ropes of straw. Stacked so high, and with the flanking bundles drooping so close to the ground, that the beasts are completely enveloped and submerged, and appear to be pushing through a tunnel of undergrowth. But they are very strong and very patient, and in as little hurry as their masters, who walk before them leading them by a rope attached to a ring through the nose. The ox should be the national emblem of Korea.

The poorer fuel-gatherers who cannot afford oxen must be their own beasts of burden. You will see them, too, bringing their loads in from the hills. They carry them on a wooden structure at the back, chair-like except that it possesses only a single pair of legs, supported by shoulder-loops of straw rope. This structure is called a *jigi*, and the load it enables a man it carry is stupendous. A station porter, for instance, will take a couple of large trunks as well as odds and ends of suit-cases at a single journey. The secret is balance. The *jigi* is set on the ground and supported at a slight forward angle by a forked staff. It is then packed, everything being tightly corded in place. The bearer backs himself against it at a squat, slips his arms through the shoulder-straps, removes the supporting staff, and using the staff to steady himself, slowly rises. Once on his feet he maintains the balance of his load by a gentle forward lean of his body, and is prepared to tramp for miles beneath a weight of two hundred pounds. When he wishes to rest he steadies himself to a squat by means of his staff, adjusts the fork of the staff in the *jigi*, and releases himself, the *jigi* remaining ready for him when he wishes to resume his journey. Indeed, the *jigi* is one of those excellent contrivances which seem to have developed like the limbs of the body itself in response to a vital demand. Korea is a land of mountains where the paths are on an everlasting gradient. A man needs his hands free, and a staff to stay him from slipping. The

THE JIGI-MAN

Chinaman's bamboo pole, with the loads slung at either end, is suitable for the plains but not for the hills. The Korean *jigi*, with its security of structure, and the ease with which it is discarded and resumed, is adapted with the perfection of something natural to the exigencies of mountain travel. . . . And in the road of the Peking Pass you will see *jigi* loads of fuel between the waiting oxen stacked half as high again as a man.

Women will pass you in the street with tubs and buckets of washing on their heads, going out to the streams in the morning and returning in the evening. If you stroll down the road to where a bridge crosses a sewer you can see them squatting in sociable groups beating their washing with wooden clubs. Beside them there may be a bucket on an open fire with the clothes boiling within. For the clothes are first ripped apart, then boiled in lye, which may be done either at home or by the waterside. After this comes the beating, which is always done in the open, even in midwinter when the ice is thick. They are beaten on a flat stone, with frequent rinsings, laid out in the sun to dry, then taken home and once more beaten, this time not to clean but to iron them, and finally, of course, put together again. It is a long process, and one would imagine fatiguing. But it is the Korean woman's social occupation. She never washes alone, but in company, and probably finds the task as enjoyable as the Western woman's knitting. Folk who confuse innovation with progress talk of soap and wringers and flat-irons, not to mention sewing-machines to save the labour of repeated rippings and joinings. But as the seams are pasted together the sewing-machine is a doubtful blessing. Also the result is so excellent, the white robes shine with so beautiful a gloss, that it seems impertinent to talk of soap and wringers and flat-irons. Besides, they are perfectly happy, these women. If Korea should ever adopt a Soviet Government the flag would be a *jigi* above crossed washing clubs on a quartered field of white and cerulean blue.

These, then, you will observe everywhere and at once, the loaded men and the washing women.

And meanwhile through another organ you will become aware of a very definite atmosphere. You will probably look askance at the sewers, perhaps keeping to the middle of the road. The sewers certainly have a savour, but not overpowering, though a little unpleasant during long spells of drought. But it is not the sewers that are distressing you ; it is the pervading reek of *kimchi*, the Korean pickle. In autumn, when the pickle is made, the reek becomes nauseating,

but throughout the year it haunts you. I have
described the smell elsewhere as that of sour
vinegar. I must confess that I have never smelt
sour vinegar. I do not even know whether
vinegar can turn sour. But if vinegar can turn
sour I should imagine it would smell like *kimchi*.
That is the best I can do for you. And it will
follow you everywhere, just as the smell of garlic
will follow you everywhere in China. It is
best to make up your mind that it is inevitable—
and dismiss it. Otherwise you may be unhappy.

You will have an eye, of course, for the stores
and the street vendors. The stores are open to
the street, usually overflowing on to the street
itself, spanning the inevitable sewer by a platform of boards. They are open from early
morning till late at night, and for seven days in
the week. But there is no strain, no fatigue, no
hurry. There is a whole family from grand-
parents to grandchildren to attend to the casual
customers, and one can sleep by day as well as
by night, and one is not enslaved to the counter.
You will see brass-ware, and brass-bound chests,
and canoe-shaped shoes in rows like boats drawn
up on the beach ; and grain in flat, round baskets,
and white cabbage stacked on the ground, and
pears and melons, and fish. Dried fish, dead
beyond redemption, as though from centuries of

smoking and salting. You must soak it a
fortnight, I am told—and I believe it—before it
is ready for use. Then, I am also told, it makes
an excellent dish ; but I prefer to reserve
judgment. Here and there are sweet-vendors,
boys mostly with trays slung from their shoulders,
shaking great scissors over slabs and twists of
inconceivable candies. These are made of
sorghum cane or barley malt, with a scattering
it may be of soya beans. As a matter of fact, the
twisted kind, a dirty cream in colour, has a
distinctly pleasant relish. Merely it is difficult
to bring oneself to the first sampling. In
season you can buy roasted chestnuts. The
vendors, boys again, set up iron braziers, known
as *wharros*, where they roast their chestnuts in
wire baskets over a charcoal fire, arranging the
nuts in little piles of a dozen or so to be sold at a
farthing the pile. Poorer folk sit by the sides of
the street before trays of wares that could be
purchased for a couple of shillings : hanks of
unbleached yarn, children's story-books gaudy
with pictures, a handful of pea-nuts, slices of
juicy, red water-melon. You might think that
if you offered to buy up such a man's stock he
would be grateful to you. But, on the contrary,
he would refuse to sell. He must retain something to continue trade. In summer you will

see women outside their doorways boiling herb
soups or frying pancakes, and men " kneading "
dough. This is really interesting. The opera-
tion requires three men. The dough, sad and
pallid, is laid in a lump on a board. Two men
with enormous mallets stand over it and pound
it strenuously, as though driving in stakes. The
third, squatting beside it, slaps it with his hand
between blows. The precise virtue of his function
I have never been able to understand. The
pounding continues for hours till the dough is
belaboured to a heavy slab. The resulting
bread is what might be expected. Your jaws
will ache with chewing, but you will never reduce
it to a consistency fit to swallow. . . . And over
the fruit and the fish and the candies, the soups
and the pancakes and the dough, the dust blows
down in a cloud and the flies settle.

The muleteers come slowly, riding on their heavy packs,
Small mules, half hidden by the loads, sweat streaming
    down their backs.
Ah ! the shouting and the straining and the pulling as they
    go,
Beaten when they move too quickly, beaten when they move
    too slow,
Like mules on the Peking highway three hundred years ago.
Beyond the city gateway, beyond the broken wall,
Where, from the shattered rampart, great blocks of stone-
    work fall,
Into the purple mountain the long road winds away.

H

Do shadows from those ramparts lean to watch at close of
    day
The lights that move and vanish along the great high-
    way. . . .

There are not many beggars here, as it is off
the main routes, but a little boy may attach
himself to you, piteously entreating for a sen :
" *Toon il-jeun ch'eupsio !* " He will be grimed and
ragged, and his face expressive of unimaginable
anguish. He will hold out a hand, bobbing up
and down from the hips, and will follow you
persistently till you satisfy him or till he spies
another more likely patron. But you will do
well to keep your money. It will not go to the
boy, but to his master who sets the child to
beg, perhaps maiming him for the purpose,
certainly in winter sending him out half naked
into the cold, to live himself on the profits.

There are other things you will see. Old men
squatting in groups smoking long pipes, chatting
together throatily, and nonchalantly rolling back
their clothing in a leisurely search for lice ; and
children with babies strapped to their backs
playing in the mud of the gutters ; and young
men stripped to the waist washing themselves
and one another, or with their mouths in a foam
vigorously scrubbing their teeth. But then, this
is not Seoul ; this is Keijo intruding again ; for

washing is an innovation from Japan. If you are fortunate you will see a funeral or a wedding ; and you will certainly see all that you are likely to of the customary costumes of the people.

The women are full-skirted and short-bodiced with bunchy enfoldings about the waist. In summer the bodices are so short that the breasts protrude beneath, for the better convenience of the babies strapped behind who can be drawn round for nourishment or comfort. If in full dress, they wear also a long robe. The hair is oiled to a black smoothness, parted down the middle, and gathered into a tight knot at the neck. In winter a curious hat appears. It is best described as two cheek-pieces joined at the front and back, but left open at the top. It is made of black figured silk, and decorated at the brow with a coloured tassel. In the extreme cold a long wadded cloth is bound round the head, covering the ears and falling to the waist. The women show little expression in their faces, except when they are angry ; though those in their twenties, with their smooth, full cheeks and their sharp, clear brows, have a certain Madonna-like placidity, not without charm. And they are boldly formed, and walk sturdily, but with little grace.

The men are enormously pantalooned, and

wear loose waistcoat-like upper garments knotted at the right breast.   Like the women, they wear a long robe when in full dress.   Their faces are long and solemn, but yielding readily to laughter. In their forties they cultivate goatee beards. They walk slowly, with a majestic dignity, erect and in perfect poise.

Yet at first, possibly, you may not notice all this, because you will be scrutinizing with an amused curiosity the men's amazing head-gear, the most patently absurd, surely, in the world. Yet there is a reason in it.   Its purpose is, to protect, not the head, but the top-knot.   When a Korean boy attains to manhood—that is, when he marries, say at fifteen or sixteen—his hair is gathered up on the top of his head into a short, tight knot.   The loose lower hairs are held in place by a band of black gauze firmly secured about the head with thongs.   Over this is a black gauze cage, within which you can see the top-knot like the first sprouting of some delicate plant sheltered from the weather.   Set on the cage, some inches above the head, is the hat itself.   It is a light structure of horsehair, some-times straw-coloured, sometimes black.   To picture its shape, imagine a child's sand castle on a large plate.   It is held in place by long, black ribbons which tie under the chin.   The

Korean's dignified walk has in it a suggestion of being conscious of this hat, as though an awkward movement or a lapse from the upright would topple it from his head.

All this you can see in the road of the Peking Pass. And nightly in the summer the street is set with stalls which are lit with lamps and lanterns, though in the city itself they are lit with electricity; and for three hours the place is white with the robes of loungers and strollers and loud with the cries of the vendors, while from within the houses comes the clatter of the ironing clappers, a noise musical, persistent, and unlocatable like the chirruping of crickets. It will ring in your ears half through the night, like a resonance of the atmosphere. It is the voice of Korea, just as the top-knot is its visible symbol and *kimchi* is its odour.

Do shadows from those ramparts lean to watch at close of
    day
The lights that move and vanish along the great highway,
As once they watched and challenged the scout of Genghis
    Khan
Who rode through these same mountains down to the river
    Hahn,
Telling of great countries and of a greater king
Beyond the purple mountains and the roadway to Peking?
Maybe that rampart echoed the song he came to sing.
Ah! long, grey road you wind away beyond the saffron sky,
Luring beyond the city gate the dreams of such as I

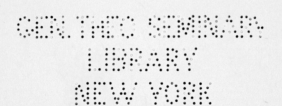

To gateways at your other end where still the merchants
  bring
Their painted fans, their carven jade, and many a silver
  ring,
To market down the road of dreams—the high road to
  Peking.

I think, after all, the Poetess is right. The
audible and the visible reveal so little of any
people. Perhaps of this people least of all.
For how should the actual concern them?
With heads arrayed in such hats they are like a
nation of priests dedicated to some fabulous and
fantastic deity of dreams.

IX

SEOUL

TURNING from the main streets you can plunge at a venture into any of the alleys— rabbit-like into a maze of burrows. For instance, having sufficiently wandered the Peking Pass and assured yourself that the Independence Arch is worth no more than a casual regard, you can take the first opening that offers on the other side of the road and make your way up to the city wall which you can see outlining the crest of the slope above you, with, if you wish as a more precise objective, the house of the Poetess which stands up in lordly detachment beside an immense Ginko tree. You can see the wall from the road, that is ; but once among the alleys it is blotted out, except for occasional glimpses in unexpected places. Yet you will expect to emerge beneath it after no very long walk, as it cannot be more than three or four hundred yards distant. But the probability is, unless you are very fortunate, that you will wander perhaps a couple of miles before you reach it, and then it

will be in some spot remote from your aim. Not
merely because of the windings of the alleys, but
because of their innumerable dead ends bringing
you up short in blind corners of walls and against
barricading doorways, compelling you to double
upon your tracks and seek for other outlets in
a growing bewilderment of disorientation. For
there is no traceable scheme in these narrow,
twisting passages. They appear as fortuitous
cracks merely between the hovels which themselves seem like some natural fungus of the soil.
Yet persist ; and do not be perturbed if the
suspicion increases upon you that you are lost.
Take the opportunity to look about you ; for
this is Seoul.

The alleys are unpaved, as you have expected,
so that with every shower they lie deep in mud.
For this emergency the Koreans have a wooden
clog, canoe-shaped, and raised several inches on
cleats ; a contrivance on which you will look
with envy. But there are steeper places where
there is no mud, because here the naked granite
pushes bare. Possibly hacked into rough steps,
very rough, and far from level, negotiable only
with extreme care in frosty weather. For this,
too, the Koreans have provided. Their ordinary
straw sandal—which you will wear yourself when
you go into the mountains—keeps them steady

A KOREAN STREET

on the steepest and most slippery slopes. But for you in your Western boots, particularly if they are rubber-soled, you are unlucky.

To one side of you is a wall, to the other an open sewer, as wide or wider than the alley itself. It is well excavated and lined with granite. The bottom runs with a thin trickle of water over a bed of muddy ooze, except in the rainy season, when it becomes a torrent. Stone slabs bridge it at intervals where doors open. Children play there; and into it latrines drain and garbage-boxes overflow.

Perhaps a beggar will pass you, lank-haired, clad in inconceivable foul rags, poking among these garbage-boxes for cabbage stalks and fish bones.

Through the open doors you can look into diminutive courtyards, set with innumerable earthenware jars of every size—reminding you of Ali Baba and the Forty Thieves—stored, you must imagine, with rice and beans and millet and, of course, *kimchi*. Facing you across the courtyard is a raised platform, roofed over by the projecting eaves of the room behind which shuts from sight the women's courtyard beyond. On this platform men may be squatting, lost in contemplation and smoke. The courtyard may be a yard square with the platform in proportion

with nothing to gaze upon but the jars or possibly
a corner of flowers ; yet except in the shelters of
the outcasts it is inevitably there, sacred to
meditation like the cloisters of a monastery.

The outer door opens, not through a single
wall, but between rooms ; to be precise, between
the kitchen and the latrine.   The kitchen is clear
to view, a mere roofed space, earth-floored, set
with a low stove by which women squat boiling
soup and rice in shallow iron pans.   There is no
oven.   And the stove-fire passes by flues under
the floors of the rooms, and the smoke issues by
chimneys no higher than your knee, filling the
alleys with a blue haze.

You may see a house or two in the building.
First a stout wooden framework held together by
wooden pegs.   The walls are mere fillings.   The
lower part, some four feet high, consists of a
muddy cement set with a patchwork of stones.
The stones are tied together with string to keep
them in place while the cement sets ; and where
an old wall begins to crumble you will see the
string exposed.   Above this base the walls are
continued for another two feet or so with a
hempen mesh filled with mud and plastered
white.   In it are inserted minute windows
opaquely papered.   Not for looking through, as
they are above eye-level for the inmates sitting

on the floor within, but merely to give light.
The roofs are of unshaped timbers, thatched for
the most part—tiles being a sign of opulence—
and projecting in deep eaves. These are so
low that you must stoop to pass beneath them.
The effect may be picturesque enough when the
plaster and cement are fresh ; but the heavy
rains play havoc with the muddy structures,
and the walls rapidly crumble. They bulge,
lean awry, crack, gape away from their frames.
But the frames hold secure, and patching is
quick and easy. Nevertheless, the squat huddling
of the hovels, the purposeless twisting of the
alleys, the sewers, the refuse, and the smoke,
give an impression of meanness and confinement,
of instability and decay, wretched, shabby and
discomforting, as though the people had somehow
lost heart.

This impression may be entirely erroneous.
For the folk are contented ; the children are
sturdy and full of play. And one must not judge
the Eastern house by Western requirements.
In the West the house is the home ; but not in
the East. In the blue Korean weather the house
need be little more than a temporary shelter
during the rains and the cold. The people live
in the streets. In the summer they cook in the
streets, sleep in the streets. At night, passing

down the alleys, you must step over prostrate bodies coiled on mats laid on the earth. Within the house it is too hot ; and there are multitudinous vermin. But lying in one's garments in the open air one keeps pleasantly warm, and moderately free from irritation. In winter, the more confined the room the cosier the atmosphere. If there is just space on the heated floor for the entire family to stretch itself, that is a completely adjusted economy. And with the whole day in the open to make up for arrears of fresh air, it is not so unsanitary as it may seem. Which brings us to a consideration of those uncovered sewers. Breeding-places for disease, you might think. Yet being uncovered they are wide to the sun. And the fact is, that during any typhoid epidemic it is the clean Japanese who die, not the dirty Koreans. There is probably a heavy infant mortality, but those who survive are surprisingly immune from pestilence. One cannot resist a certain sceptical questioning of our medicine and sanitation which barricade us behind a timid cleanliness, outside of which, poor weaklings that we have become, it grows increasingly dangerous to stray. Yet that is not the complete truth either. For the Japanese have banished smallpox and cholera from which even the Koreans were not immune.

Here among the alleys, then, you are at the heart of Seoul. And you need not feel the least uneasiness. No one will molest you, unless to be greeted by the children as you pass with shrill cries of " Goo-bye ! " constitutes a molestation. An unaccompanied lady at night is as secure here as in her own home. But squalid as the alleys may appear, do not imagine that you are in the slums. This represents the city's normal level. There are grades above it, and there are grades below.

The grades above I associate with a certain Mr. Yi. He was brought to me one day by a student of mine. He had heard about me, he said, with much bowing—to be precise, he had heard that I was " clevah teachah," which I modestly denied—and he wished to make my " ácquaintánce." For what possible reason I haven't yet been able to conceive ; except that one rapidly came to suspect all such seekers of acqauintance of desiring to improve their English, and one avoided familiarity with what polite evasions one could. But I didn't avoid Mr. Yi. Perhaps he was too tenacious. Or perhaps I spied in his companionship an advantage to myself. Because he invited me to his summer-house outside the city wall, and promised me *entrées*, besides, otherwise denied me. He was obviously a youth of means, and something of a dandy. He came dressed in Western style, in a white drill " two-piece " suit as the summer had already set in. He wore gold rings on his fingers, a jewelled tie-pin, and a flower in his buttonhole. His full face, clear and soft of skin, pinkly tinted, and no more than a shade darker than my own, showed him well fed and unaccustomed to labour. In fact, he had something of the sleek *embonpoint* of a silkworm about to cast its sixth skin. Yet he was clearly uncomfortable. He kept his fan in a constant flutter, opening his coat and easing his collar away from his neck. However, he was very amiable ; and I readily accepted his invitation.

He took me to a point to the north-east of the city, just outside the wall, which we scaled by a breach. Here I found a romantic valley, the slopes clothed in twisted pine, where a narrow path followed the windings of a stream which flowed crystal-clear among rocks. It proved to be a paradise of summer-houses to which Mr. Yi possessed some mysterious right of entry. He had merely to stand at a gate and clap his hands, and a servant appeared, bowed, threw the gate wide, and ushered us in. We followed enchanting paths among trees and boulders, every more picturesque corner set with a pavilion where one could repose in shade and admire the savage

A SUMMER RETREAT

attitude of some ancient pine, the strenuous poise
of some enormous rock, the stillness of a deep
pool, the plunging of a cascade. And the main
house itself would possess something of this fairy
quality of the surrounding gardens. It was
built as always on the courtyard plan. But the
courtyards were daintily planted with flowering
shrubs, set with stone lanterns, laid with straight,
flagged paths possibly with a goldfish pool in
the centre. Outside was the beauty of nature.
Within was the beauty of art. Beauty tamed and
ordered to flatter some more subtle sense than a
mere rapturous response to the splendid and the
uncouth. But in either case, beauty to be contemplated and admired. For enclosing the
courtyards, or perhaps facing them to one end
only, were verandaed rooms where one could sit
as in the pavilions to gaze and meditate. And
above one's head the sweeping tiled roofs curved
up with an airy lift like a bird's wings.

But amusement was not entirely æsthetic.
There were stages for the dancing-girls, a
necessary seasoning to any pleasure.

As for Mr. Yi, he was not master himself of
such splendour. His own house was a miniature
affair, his courtyard a confined enclosure possess-
ing a single persimmon tree, and his garden had
been given over to a vineyard. But we sat on

the veranda and talked together, and ate nameless delicacies and drank wine, and could imagine
ourselves if we wished in one of those more
spacious pavilions with the dancing-girls posing
for us in long-sleeved silken robes and black
coils of jewelled hair.

But Seoul has still one sight for you. To see it
in its full significance you should make your
visit in the winter. On the surrounding hills,
particularly to the west, the homeless folk gather
and dig holes in the earth, covering them with
rags and mats. Entire families live in these
holes, begging their bread by day or grubbing it
from the garbage-boxes. And they light fires
with such scrapings of leaves as they can gather,
huddling close for warmth in an atmosphere
thick with smoke. Yet they endure the winter,
though some of them die. One pities them, of
course ; it is impossible not to. But it is wise to
avoid indignation. Conditions may be against
them. They may be victims of a social system.
But the Koreans are so completely Christian in
the one respect of taking no thought for the
morrow that you may be certain that many of
these people have sold their houses during the
summer to satisfy a temporary craving for a
bicycle or a pair of Western boots, or simply to
indulge in one evening of glorious debauch ; and

THE HOMES OF THE SQUATTERS

now they are without shelter. Besides, on waste land you can see the mud hovels of more provident squatters. They also were homeless ; but they have grown a crop of millet in the thin soil of the hills, and at the expense of a few days' labour have put up at least a room with a roof, no very artistic affair, being patched with old boxes and mats and flattened oil tins, but large enough to store a jar or two of grain in and to sleep with stretched-out limbs. These hole-dwellers could presumably do the same. But, theorize as you wish, there they are, the unfortunate and the failures. You can see them by their holes amid a litter of refuse sorting out the revolting offal they have gathered from the streets. And you will contrast them, inevitably, with the wealthy æsthetes to whom nature is a spectacle to be contemplated in detached serenity. But that demands comfort and a full stomach.

After all, in essentials, does the East differ so much from the West ? In Korea the rich man and the poor have precisely the same social sense as their counterparts in England.

So back to the alleys, and you will find those low, thatched houses by comparison unexpectedly cheerful and commodious. You will not think of them now as hovels, but as bourgeois villas, substantial, smug and prim.

I

X

SHOPS AND SHOPPING

YOU will see many tailors, both Japanese and Korean, but you will patronize the China-man, Yuan Tai. This Celestial, whose own trousers divide six inches too low and termi-nate six inches too high and are, moreover, to all appearance reversible, will produce for you anything from a dress-suit to a pair of hiking shorts of irreproachable shape and fit. And having a monopoly of these things among the foreigners he will not charge you more than fifty per cent. above European prices. His monopoly is due not merely to his own dexterity, but to the incompetence of his competitors. Which might tempt one from insignificant sartorial considerations to considerations of racial moment. The Japanese are universally credited with a genius for imitation. As a nation of imitators they are unsurpassed, but as individuals they make a poor second to the Chinese. The Japanese will organize a business on Western lines, but the Chinaman makes the better

mason, carpenter, bricklayer, tailor, bootmaker.
For you will also go to the Chinaman, Mei Wha,
for your boots. But perhaps the most delightful
characteristic of the Chinese workman is that he
is never without a contrivance or a remedy.
Where the Korean and the Japanese will shake
their heads with a smiling, " Cannot. I am
sorry for you," the Chinaman always " Can do."
Whether to make or to mend, he is equally
resourceful, and when he is baffled it means
simply that the problem you have set him is
beyond all human ingenuity. The lover's task in
the old English song, " to make a cambric shirt
without any needle or needle-work," would not
have disconcerted him ; and he would have put
Humpty-Dumpty together again with a few rivets.

When the great bronze bell arrived from
Loughborough for the English Cathedral in
Keijo, the architect saw no hope of hauling it
into place without bringing the whole belfry
down with a crash. But the Chinese workmen
were not dismayed by his theoretic resistances and
strains. They rigged up a crude engine of ropes
and beams which sent the architect running for
safety. He washed his hands of the affair, and
retired into hiding, he told me, in a nervous
prostration. But when he ventured forth again
the bell was serenely installed.

But your most delightful dealings with the Chinese will be your bargainings with the " Laceman." To enjoy this to the full you should spend a few weeks at the foreign holiday resort at Wonsan Beach. The summer heat will drive you from the city to the mountains or the sea, and unless you leave the country you won't do much better than Wonsan. The foreigners have purchased a long stretch of beach there in a picturesque bay, set with islands, backed by mountains, and have built wooden holiday shanties among a plantation of low pines. The shanties consist largely of windows, unglazed, but provided with shutters against the rain, and netted against mosquitoes. Yet the mosquitoes penetrate, and it is as well to have a supply of incense-sticks to burn in the evening. There is a meeting-hall on the Beach, a boarding-house, tennis courts, a golf course, and a Korean junk in attendance for bathers. The atmosphere is somewhat female and very missionary, as, other than missionaries, there are comparatively few foreigners in Korea. Alcohol is prohibited, tobacco is grudgingly tolerated, and " there is a sentiment against bathing on Sunday." The weather in the summer alternates between scorching suns and drenching rains. On clear days the heat sets in at eight in the morning ;

but usually at ten a relieving breeze springs up. If not, there is no alternative but to creep into such shade as the pines afford and refrain from all motion. Of course one can bathe, but the hundred yards or so to the sea is a labour not to be too frequently undertaken, and to remain on the sand, which scorches your feet through your shoes and which offers not a single inch of shelter, is unthinkable. However, the bathing, when you do venture to the water, is superb. There is no tide. The sea is warm and transparent, glass-smooth in calm weather, and after a sudden typhoon heaved into magnificent rollers which you can ride like horses. Also, the nights are invariably cool. But you see, although there are tennis courts and a golf course, there is little opportunity for exercise except before breakfast and after supper. The heat will not permit it. For occupation there is bridge for the ungodly, and ice-cream tea-parties for both ungodly and devout. There is, moreover, a weekly concert in the meeting-hall, very amateur but very well meant, which provides a certain unintentional comic relief. But such a programme leaves weary gaps. And this is why one welcomes the Lace-man.

He comes to you drowsing on your hammock ; or you hear his voice under the window, " Lady

wantee lace ? " You summon him. He squats
on his haunches before you, his lean face in a
charming smile, and unslings the two packages
from either end of his bamboo shoulder-pole,
while the air fills with the reek of garlic. He
carefully unwraps his wares, displaying them for
you one by one, refolding them and setting them
aside. Not lace alone, but five o'clock tea-
cloths daintily embroidered with gateways and
pagodas and diminutive figures of Celestials,
with napkins to match, other cloths for nameless
inutilities ornate with immense golden dragons,
table-runners and cushion-covers in blue silken
tapestries, long gowns of pongee silk. You select
an article, lay it apart ; another ; your pile
grows ; you compare, consider. There is no
hurry. Eventually you offer a price. The Lace-
man breaks into a bright laugh as though at a
merry jest, and begins to pack up his goods.
" Then how much ? " you ask. He doubles your
figure. You increase your offer a fraction ; he
descends a fraction to meet you. It is now your
turn to make a stand. " You too dear," you
say ; and you pick up a book and assume a
complete indifference. He assails you, shaking
the articles at you, crying, " How muchee ?
How muchee ? Last price how muchee ? "
You repeat your figure, which he greets with

another laugh, but this time edged with scorn.
"No can do," he declares. He becomes
plaintive : "Me velly poor man. You velly
rich lady. You number one rich lady. You
plenty money. How muchee? Last price how
muchee?" You remain firm. He begins to
pack up his goods again, perhaps really packs
them up, perhaps leaves the house. But he
returns ; if not the same day, then the next, and
the day after, till the bargain is concluded.
Concluded, if you are obstinate, at your own
terms. At the end he makes semblance of
elaborate calculations, then throws the articles
at you with a gesture of despair : " Velly cheaf ;
too cheaf. Me lose plenty money." And the
following day you hear his voice again, " Lady
wantee lace ? " Of course you chide him archly,
" But last time you lose plenty money, why you
come again ? " . . . It is an excellent pastime.

In much the same manner Korean hawkers
besiege you in your city home ; but there time
is of more account, and the charm has gone.
Most patient people, these hawkers. They do
not argue with you, do not overwhelm you with
pitiful entreaties. They squat at your door for
an hour or so until somehow they become
admitted. Then they spread their wares over
the floor of your vestibule—brass bowls, brass-

bound boxes, boxes of black lacquer inlaid with mother-of-pearl, strings of amber beads— squatting beside them without a word, waiting until some one comes to examine them. They will wait a whole morning, and even then perhaps no purchaser appears. Or if you take pity on the poor man and look over his stock he makes little effort to sell. He doesn't belaud his wares. He suggests no imaginary needs, indicates nothing for your inspection. And convinced at long last that there is to be no trade he packs up in leisurely apathy and moves on to the next house. But it doesn't seem to matter.

For ordinary purposes you patronize the Japanese shops in the Hon Machi. There is a sort of Woolworth's there, known as the H Store, and a sort of Selfridge's, Mitsukoshi. It was at the H store that my wife was once greeted by an affable assistant with the perplexing formula, " Good morning. How are you ? I am sorry for you." But after this his English failed. There is also a Beauty Shop which, wise in foreign taste, sets little, nude images in the window, which the natives find sniggeringly intriguing ; and a music shop which advertises " orugans " and " guramohons," usually crowded about the doorway with kimonoed figures intent on a stridency of radio music broadcast from the local J.O.D.K. (Jéee Awww Deee Kéee). The silk stores are always picturesque with a display of materials in intricate, bright, flowered designs. When the Girls' Festival draws round in May there are innumerable windows set with dolls arrayed in meticulous imitation of the old Japanese Court dresses ; miracles of delicate craftsmanship. And always at any festival season there are displays of flower arrangement. But Keijo is not Peking ; it is not even Tokyo. There is little to buy.

At Christmas, however, you may win a prize. I know a lady who won a prize. For every yen's worth of goods that you buy you receive a ticket. You take your ticket to a stall, where there are all sorts of attractive articles on view, and having surrendered your ticket you plunge your hand into a box and withdraw a lottery number. For this you usually receive a packet of caramels. I have received dozens of packets of caramels. But I know a lady who won a first prize. The prize was worth four pounds. But it was wasted on her. For she was a very prim missionary spinster, and the prize was a barrel of Japanese wine.

She said she didn't drink wine, and asked if she might have the equivalent in goods. But that was quite impossible. It was against police regulations, which stated that a prize-winner must receive his prize.

Which puts me in mind of another story of police regulations, not entirely irrelevant, because connected with this same street. It is a long, narrow street, gay with lanterns, with artificial cherry-blossom in spring and maple-leaf in autumn, and its hard surface perpetually ringing with the " crank-cronk " of Japanese clogs. Bicycles used to be a danger before they were prohibited, and rickshas are still an annoyance. Once cars were permitted, but they have been forbidden now for some time. When that regulation was first made, a foreigner, unaware of it, drove into the street, but was of course stopped by a policeman. Being informed of the new regulation he backed out. But the policeman had not finished with him.

" That is a fine of four yen," he said.

Without protest the foreigner paid the four yen. But even so the policeman had not finished.

" For you," he said, " it will be eight yen ; for not only did you drive in, but you also drove out."

I should like to tell you, too, of the Severance Hospital Drug Store. Though this belongs to the Severance Hospital—a large missionary hospital—it is under Korean management. The manager, trained abroad, once complained to

my wife, who was buying some Lux, that unfortunately he could not charge her so much now
as he used to do because, as the Japanese stores
had also taken to selling Lux, he could no longer
fix his own price, in fact he had had to reduce
his price from thirty-five sen to twenty-eight.
He spoke pathetically, and expected my wife to
sympathize.   Once, too, I went to this same store
to buy some disinfectant. ⟨My wee son was
unwell, and as my wife and I were obliged to
share a room with him we thought it advisable to
spray the air. I explained my needs to the
assistant. He vanished for consultation with the
manager, and reappeared some fifteen minutes
later with some Flit.

" This will kill flies," I said, " but will it kill
germs ? "

He didn't know, so vanished for a second
consultation, and returned to say that he was
very sorry but it wouldn't kill germs.

" Then it's no good for my purpose," I said.

" No good," he agreed.

" Well, then," I told him, " let me have something that *will* kill germs."

He vanished a third time. He was away at
least half an hour. But this time he seemed to
have been successful. He presented me with a
bottle of liquid.

" This will kill germs," he declared.

" What is it ? " I asked.

" I think, formaldehyde," he answered.

I might have taken it in my ignorance, but I happened to have memories of formaldehyde, memories of the spraying of billets during the war. My particular memory was that for two hours after the spraying no one could enter the billets, and even after two hours it was distressing for the nose and eyes. I expressed my doubts to the assistant.

" Can I use this while the patient is in the room ? " I asked. This occasioned a fourth disappearance. He returned for the last time.

" Very sorry," he said. " This will kill germs, but it will also kill the patient."

There were occasions when tourists came to visit Keijo. They came in a sudden swarm, and the next day had vanished. Usually they came in a ship named the " Resolute." On one such occasion one of the Severance doctors suggested to the manager of the drug store that he might make a special display to attract the patronage of the " Resolute " tourists. When the ship arrived the doctor discovered a couple of ladies of his acquaintance, and naturally enough escorted them over the hospital, completing the inspection with a visit to the drug store. Expecting an imposing display, he was prepared to usher the ladies in with a certain triumphant flourish. But facing him on the front door he saw an enormous placard :

WELCOME

TO THE

RESOLUTE

WE SELL

KOTEX

XI

SCHOOLS

I HAVE referred to myself both as a teacher at a school and a professor at a university. I was both, because my school was the Preparatory School of the Keijo Imperial University, and the teachers there were entitled to style themselves professors. This does not mean that I held a chair, nor even that I lectured on English Literature. The school was of high-school standard merely—though the boys were mostly in their twenties and many of them were married—and I was occupied quite humbly in teaching English conversation and composition. I say " teaching " to indicate an aim rather than an achievement, because whenever I was asked —chiefly by zealous American missionary educators—what I taught my students, my unvarying, and entirely truthful, reply was " Nothing." This always caused consternation. It checked the mirth of innocently festive reunions in Japanese restaurants and shocked into silence whole dinner tables. I suppose there was a

suggestion in it of an attitude flagrantly un-
principled. Until I explained. The boys came
to me with anything from five to ten years of
English study behind them, but under the
Japanese. To build on this foundation would
have been like building on a ditchful of loose
rubble. Their pronunciation was so original
that to make me understand they were obliged to
repeat their remarks to me two or three times and
word by word, even letter by letter ; and my
pronunciation seemed to them so ludicrous that
it sent them into violent fits of laughter. So it
took us quite a long time to adjust ourselves to
each other, on a basis of mutual forbearance.
There was no unpleasantness. The students were
very considerate. After all, coming from the
other side of the world it was natural that I
should have picked up some curious habits of
speech. And we drifted finally into the tacit
agreement that I might pronounce in my own
insular way, provided I did not insist on their
imitating me. But it was all very jolly, because
when the fog of dullness was settling over a
lesson I would fix on something a student had
said, and say, " Now in England we would
pronounce it like this " ; and the gush of unintelligible noises that I emitted would dissipate
the dullness on a roar of delight.

It was from a sense of duty rather than with
any anticipation of pleasure that I visited other
schools. Indeed, I found it was part of my normal
programme for which I was made a generous
travelling allowance by the authorities. It is
the Japanese practice, which might well be
adopted in England, to send their teachers
frequently on visiting tours to schools both in
their own and in foreign countries. I also was
sent on such a tour ; but that was in Japan
proper, not in Korea. But quite on my own
I looked up a school or two in the capital, both
Japanese and American. At the Normal School,
where boys were being trained as teachers, I
listened to an English lady teaching English to
a class of young children. This was an experiment. The Japanese refuse to be convinced that
the English teacher can do more effective work
in the early than in the later stages of the
language. At present teachers are engaged from
England, on extremely generous salaries, for the
High Schools and the Universities only ; with
the result that I have mentioned. However,
here was a definite experiment. The Principal
of the school, a very fat man of frog-like dignity,
who awed me into speechless insignificance,
seemed fond of experiments. There were no
punishments at his school, he told me. That

might very well be, I thought, since a visit to
his study should be sufficient to intimidate the
most obstreperous ; but he added that of course
it was necessary occasionally to expel a boy from
the school. However, apart from that single
trifling resource, which would merely ruin the
culprit's career, there were no punishments.
And here was another experiment, allowing
English to be taught to children by an English
teacher. His somewhat condescending manner
suggested that of course the experiment would
be a failure, but it was worth making merely to
establish that. But if I know the English lady
in question, and I know her pretty well, the
experiment will not be a failure. She is very
persevering, and holds her opinions with an
unshakable fortitude. I argued with her for a
long time on the pronunciation of " Saturday."
She maintained that the Japanese and Koreans
should be taught to pronounce it " Sat-ur-day."
I maintained that no Englishman ever said
" Sat-ur-day," but " Sáturdy," that it was to
be found so, though in phonetic symbols, in
standard dictionaries of pronunciation, that in
fact she was falling into the same error as the
Japanese, who base their teaching on the theory
of an obsolete orthography instead of on the
practice of living people. I was very logical,

K

and expressed myself well. But, you know, I couldn't convince her. Still, we only argued, we didn't quarrel. It wouldn't have been safe, as at that moment I was balancing a teacup on one knee and a plate piled with cake and sandwiches on the other. And to prove that we didn't quarrel I was invited to lunch. " When shall I come ? " I asked.

" Why, let me see," the lady replied, " do you think you could manage Sáturdy ? "

Once, quite by accident, I visited another school. At least, it was hardly a visit as I merely looked in through a window. It was during a walk in the country. Passing through a village of some twenty hovels I heard a persistent and resolute shouting. The effect was something of what might be expected if half a dozen clarionetists, with their instruments all in disaccord, selected each a different note and maintained it in strenuous rivalry against the rest. Looking through the window of the particular hovel from which this clamour emanated, I saw six little boys squatting on the floor, each with a book before him inscribed with large Chinese characters, each crying out the characters at the full strength of his lungs. They sat in two rows facing each other, but judging by the concentrated anguish of their faces they were

entirely oblivious of their fellows. Entirely
oblivious of me too, in spite of my foreign face
framed so unexpectedly in the tiny window. But
perhaps not so oblivious of their master, a bearded
Korean dressed in the native white robe with
little horsehair hat complete, who sat to one end
surveying them with grave severity. So, I
thought, turning away, in spite of our fine new
education the old learning still persists. And at
the back of my mind I always have that picture.
It mingles with the memory of Yu See Kuk in
our inn at Kyung Ju rhapsodizing in broken
English on the beauty of the Chinese Classics,
and complaining that, being obliged to study
them in the Japanese version, the beauty was
outraged, whereas studied in the Korean . . .
But I know nothing of that. But what I do know
is that the Chinese Classics still hold their place.
They are the Virgil and the Homer of the East,
the Lucretius and the Plato. Their acquisition
is a gentlemanly accomplishment, exactly like
the acquisition of Latin and Greek in the West.
Exactly, because their purpose seems to be to
confer the distinction of inutility on a man and
to furnish him with apt quotations completely
divorced from reality, just as " Dulce et decorum
est pro patria mori " is heard frequently in the
lecture-hall but never on the battlefield. But

the peculiar thing is this : Latin and Greek do provide a harmonious background for Western education, but the Chinese Classics do not. Yet they are still an essential part of the curriculum. Perhaps there is a hint of an explanation of the failure of Western education in the East. Because it is a failure.

Yet there is no lack of method. The Japanese schools, in Korea as well as in Japan proper, are divided into Primary, Middle and High, leading to the University. At present there is only one university in Korea, for men, not women. The schools are practically free, even to the University —at my own school I was told the students' fees just covered the coal bill—and attendance will be compulsory up to Middle School standard as soon as sufficient schools have been provided. At the junior schools the teaching is done in Japanese, except in the so-called Common Schools which are attended by the Korean children who cannot yet speak Japanese. At the High Schools and University entrance is by competitive examination. And these, you will be surprised to read, are only open to those " who speak the national language." But then, the " national language " of Korea is Japanese ! However, the distinction is one of ability, not as in England one of class and wealth. Which, of course, is to the good. There are also commercial schools and agricultural schools and industrial schools and medical schools, the Government hospital in the capital being incorporated in the University. The teachers are trained in special institutions, and the High School teachers are nearly all sent abroad ; to England for language, to Germany for medicine, to France for law. But as it is almost impossible for a Korean to become a High School teacher, this privilege is practically monopolized by the Japanese. The buildings are extremely up-to-date, even if hideous, and excellently equipped. Indeed, one wonders how such an enormous structure of free education is financed. Especially when one reckons up the number of the staff and servants. A school of three or four hundred pupils will have some half-dozen clerks in the office, perhaps two messengers, a boy in permanent attendance in the staff room, odd men and women for cooking and charring, a chauffeur for the school car, possibly a librarian. And at a university dinner which I attended—there are some seven hundred students in the University—I counted four hundred professors. Remember, too, that in Korea a teacher receives forty per cent. above his Japanese salary to compensate him for being in exile, and is retired on a pension, if he wishes, at the end of ten years. Still, there it is, a highly efficient organization, and clearly not cramped for funds.

It is, as you have probably gathered, State controlled. The control is ultra-Prussian in its completeness, and is outwardly expressed by the uniform worn during a boy's entire school and university career. Indeed, Japanese education is a tool in the hands of the Government. The aim is to shape the nation on a definite plan for a definite purpose. I remember one day sitting next to Pal Sung Yi in a tram, compressed together by the crowded students on their way to school. I had an attaché-case on my knees, with a book open on the case. I was attempting to read, in fact I was succeeding, because long habit had inured me to the conditions of the Korean tram. To be precise, I was reading " La Vie de Jeanne D'Arc," which would be absorbing in any circumstances. But Pal Sung Yi interrupted me. He also had a book, I noticed. He was studying the history of England, he told me, about William the Conqueror, the Battle of Hastings. The peculiar smile on his softly pouting lips expressed an ironical bewilderment. I knew a question was to come. The burden of it was, why do the English allow the story of Hastings to be recorded in their histories?

I had been so lost in the trial of Jeanne that I did not immediately see the point of the question.

" Why," I said, " it happened."

Pal Sung Yi's reply made that crowded and jolting tram for me the scene of an unforgettable illumination.

" But it was so shameful," he said.

One was left to surmise that the Japanese history was taught on the principle that shameful things must be repressed, that nothing must be admitted which did not redound to the national glory. Distorted in this way, history may be an effective vehicle for Government propaganda. As in the East it is.

When I visited the American mission school I found the Principal disturbed by the problem of registration. I was to find other missionary educators disturbed by the same problem. If a school remained unregistered it would lose all standing, and the pupils would leave, knowing quite well that as old scholars of such a school they would stand no chance of an official post. But to register, quite apart from being open to continual inspection and being obliged to comply with an abundance of petty regulations, meant that the Government syllabus must be followed, that equipment must be kept to standard—at the Mission expense—that a certain proportion of the teachers must be Japanese, including the teachers of history and ethics, that religious instruction must not be compulsory, and must not be given at all during school hours. It was very awkward. It meant that America would be sending money to Korea to help foot the bill of Japanese State education, which is directly opposed both in method and principle to the education of America. Yet most of the mission schools have registered, though I can't for the life of me see why they don't close down.

But that's how it is.

Yet beneath the crust of this efficient organization and deliberate control there is an essential rottenness. The science students, for instance, learn Latin, the University prospectus will tell you. I used to teach that Latin. The students came to me one hour a week for one year. Say thirty-five periods in all. And I taught in English, of course, which they could barely understand. French is taught to the law students —I know the teacher—in something the same way. The students are examined terminally. But I was told, when I handed in my first term's results, that the marks were too low. Next term, please, would I make them higher. I made them higher, and all was well. I came to see that my standard must be not from nought to a hundred, with the century a dim ideal, but from forty to a hundred, with the century a frequent realization. Yet all those terminal papers are fastened in bundles and signed and labelled and kept for reference in the school archives.

That is one side.

The other is more serious still. The very people whom the State is so anxious to mould into compliance, or rather to forge into a national weapon, are the ones who most readily rebel. I don't refer merely to the school strikes, though these may be important enough to involve the military. The real bogy of Japan is communism, known as " dangerous thought," and the most fertile field for communism is the students. As Primary and Middle School boys they believe zealously enough that the first Japanese Emperor descended from heaven seven hundred years before Christ, they believe in the divinity of the reigning Emperor and would religiously sacrifice their lives for his sake ; but in the High School and the University they learn of the Old Stone Man and they study biology and evolution, and faith yields to doubt, and doubt becomes definite denial. Their carefully expurgated history cannot stand the test of scientific investigation ; their ancient ethic of obedience to one's parents, to one's ancestors, or complete subservience to the throne, is shaken by the study of Western literature, which reveals to them a more human and a more liberal code. Add to this, that the Easterner's conception of learning is a means to obtaining official appointments, but that with education becoming universal, as it already is in Japan, as it soon will be in Korea, there are not nearly enough appointments, official or otherwise, to go round, and you can see that the High Schools and the Universities are aggravating the problem of unemployment ; aggravating it in a particularly insidious way by loosing upon a simple and primitive people an increasing band of conceited young men, talented in their own manner, with a prestige of learning, naturally fluent and forceful in speech, and hankering for an upheaval in the expectation of plunder in the form of lucrative offices in the new State that is to be. This has already brought disaster to China. It is a menace in Japan and Korea. Can one be surprised that the police are instructed to arrest at sight anyone suspected of " dangerous thought " ?

It is all very sad, because the intention behind it is so excellent. To create a nation of enlightened fanatics is a conception both original and sublime. Merely it has the trifling drawback of being impossible. But, after all, Korea is a country of farmers. Why bother them with our Western learning, so fruitful of unsettlement, so ill-adapted to their needs? It might even be better to return to that little village school with the half-dozen scholars crying out their characters at the full stretch of their lungs beneath the vigilant, grave eyes of their master.

But of course you will tell me that one can't put the clock back. Possibly not ; but I should like to know for which hour the alarm is set.

XII

THE CASE OF MARY PAK

HER name wasn't Mary Pak at all, but decency demands a certain disguise. However, her first name was Western, and Mary may very well stand for it. Her family name was, of course, Korean. For some months she was a fellow lodger of mine. We talked frequently together, having common interests but divergent opinions. Which makes for conversation more abundantly than agreement.

She was so vital a personality that it seems unfair to make of her a " case." Yet she was a case. Expressed at its simplest her case was this : educated in America from the age of seven she returned to Korea at twenty-one, both in manner and at heart an alien, yet was expected by her people to resume her place in the family exactly like a Korean woman. This would have been difficult enough as a mere change of habits ; for instance, long skirts, a strange diet, sitting and sleeping on the floor. But it demanded more than this ; it demanded a change of psychology, which was impossible. The girl didn't know two words of her native tongue. When she visited her people they conversed in English. This was a barrier in itself. Surmountable, of course, if considered simply as a question of language. But it was a question of adjustment to life, of background, of equipment, of attitude. Her outlook was that of an American girl.

Then there were other complications. She had been taken to America by missionaries— to be exact, by my hosts, which accounts for our lodging in the same household. Yet she was outspokenly hostile to missions. If she had been politic enough to conceal her hostility many excellent appointments would have offered themselves for her selection. But she refused to bow her head in the House of Rimmon. Which further incensed her people, staunchly Christian. Her father, one of the wealthiest men in Korea, and probably quite the cleverest, stopped all supplies, leaving the girl the alternatives of returning to home duties, living on charity, or cutting herself adrift from family and friends and making such way for herself as she could. The last, you must understand, no easy matter for an Eastern woman. Yet it was eventually this course that she chose.

How we first came to cross swords I can't quite

remember. What I do remember is that I found myself committed to a most astonishing attitude. I became an ardent champion of imperialism, of strong and ruthless Government, of " the white man's burden," of the duty of the powerful to rule the weak for their own good. I was driven into this position as into the last stronghold of an invaded land by Mary Pak's pugnacious advocacy of Freedom. By which she meant the right of the individual to follow his particular crazes in utter disregard of the opinion of his fellows, the demands of custom, the good of his country, or the uplift of the world.

" What do you mean," she asked me, " by the uplift of the world ? "

Well, after all, what did I mean ? The words sounded simple enough, but they defied me to expound them. And she found it quite easy— I should have found it quite easy myself—to dismiss my specific examples of uplift as mere tinkerings and patchings of doubtful benefit if not of definite harm. It was intolerable to be obliged to defend myself against the very cynicisms which I delighted in pitting against others. But it was an amusing exercise in dialectics, and I came to enjoy it.

The burden of her complaint was that life demanded liberty, but that custom enclosed the individual within limiting prohibitions. She was responsible to herself, wasn't she? Then why shouldn't she satisfy her tastes, her impulses, her needs? Of course I entirely sympathized with her. If she had been more beautiful she might have been a dangerous opponent. But her rather screwed-up face and shrill voice fortified a man's resistance. I was cruel enough to tell her to satisfy her needs and see what came of it. She grew angry, which made her less attractive than ever. Couldn't I see? That was just the point. The world had conspired against the individual. And I was part of the world. I was too timid to rebel. Which was probably quite true. But I gave such face of wisdom as I could to my timidity.

"You must remember," I said, "that the test of conduct is not its application to one but its application to all," which, though I hated the priggishness of it, was also quite true.

But I could understand well enough her fierce individualism. She was cut off from her countrymen by her Western upbringing, and from her Western upbringing by her Eastern blood. Moreover, she was a woman. For a man with her training, and incidentally with her brains, life would have been easy. Whatever career he had chosen, he would have possessed an enormous advantage over his fellows. And marriage would have offered no difficulty, the Easterner, however westernized, requiring little more than a woman in the background to order his house and provide him with sons. But for Mary Pak marriage to a Korean was unthinkable, to a foreigner impossible. Which drove her to the emphatic declaration, unnecessarily repetitive, that marriage was slavery. She would never marry ; she needed to be free. She was forced to her individualistic creed ; she was so absolutely alone.

It was more to the point when the debate turned on Korea.

Here I had an unexpected ally, as my brother came over from China, his mind somewhat bitterly occupied with the disastrous results there of the gospel of liberty and the subversion of government. It was natural that Mary Pak should see in her people a magnified example of her own case. The Japanese imposed their laws on the Koreans without the Koreans' consent. Her country was justified in its resentment, would be justified, if it had the power, in resistance. Indeed, the girl manifested sufficient " dangerous thought " to lodge her in jail, I should imagine, for the rest of her life. At this time I knew little enough of the benefits of the Japanese rule, and wasn't qualified to reply, but my brother could quote China. Liberty under the Chinese nationalists meant liberty for the idle to rob the industrious, for the strong to rob the weak. It was simply that the Government had been removed and bandits sprang up like weeds. But then, Mary Pak countered, shrilly ironical, we were English ; of course we defended the Japanese, because we were doing exactly the same in India as the Japanese were doing in Korea. But what right had we in India? What right had we to impose our regulations on the Indians against their will? We had made them a nation of slaves.

" Certainly," my brother said, " we don't let them burn their widows."

Of course the debates—they were innumerable, blazing up at the least provocation—resulted in no conclusion. But they clarified for me the tangled problem of dominance and subserviency. Not that they solved the problem—I don't believe that there is a solution—but they established certain abstract and universal principles on which any theory of Government must be based. Principles which are commonplaces in the West, but not in the East. As, for instance, that without order there can be no liberty ; that liberty is not the birth of a moment, but of the

L

labour of generations.   Commonplaces, I repeat ;
yet to the Korean mind paradoxes and contra-
dictions.   Even to Mary Pak ; intellectually of
the West, but emotionally of the East.   To her,
liberty and order (which she called restriction)
were fundamentally opposed ; and being a gift
of nature, like the sun and the open air, liberty
needed no cultivation, no preparation.   Simply
one behaved as one pleased, and one was free.
And perhaps it is that spirit, rather than national
resentment, that is thwarting the work of the
Japanese Government in Korea.

One admits the red tape, of course.   One
admits the petty officiousness, even the
favouritism and the injustice.   But the fact
remains that Japan found Korea in a state of
apathetic exhaustion due partly at least, and
many will declare entirely, to the misrule of the
native Korean Court, and from this apathetic
exhaustion Japan is striving, with all her resources
of ingenuity and power, to lift the country to the
level of a modern nation.   She has created roads,
railways, postal and telegraph services, universal
electric lighting, sanitation.   Whether these
things are benefits or not, they are now there.
She has distributed wholesale, and free, the
best breeds of fowls, so that the Korean egg is no
longer a meagre thing hardly worth the shelling

for the meat within, but has both quality and size. She has planted fruit-trees on the hill-sides where rice cannot grow. She has set aside spaces for experimental farms. She has irrigated waste land, is rapidly damming the rivers and building cisterns to obviate both flood and drought. She is afforesting the hills, which, left to themselves, the Koreans completely denuded except in the grounds of palaces and temples and royal tombs. But all the Korean sees is that whereas water was free he must now pay three yen (six shillings) a year, and that he may only chop such wood for his house and his fire as the authorities permit. And it is useless to tell him that for six shillings a year he has perhaps a doubled rice-crop, and is completely relieved of the menace of famine ; and that, although wood-cutting is restricted, at least he has wood to cut, whereas before he had nothing but the yearly shrub that sprouted on the mountains.

Well, what can you do with such a people ? One can sympathize with the Japanese irritation ; indeed, one wonders why they do not retire and leave the Koreans to themselves. The obvious answer to that is that Korea is strategically necessary and commercially profitable. But there is another answer, a more fundamental one ; the answer which Japan, sincerely or not, prefers to make. The answer, indeed, which the British make when questioned concerning India. Left to themselves the Koreans would rot, which would affect not Korea alone but the whole world. Not that Korea is very vast or very vital. To allow India to rot, for instance, would be a much more serious proposition. But the principle is the same. Eventually all policy must become, as it is becoming, world-wide. No nation, however insignificant, however mean its contribution to mankind, can be allowed to fall into neglect and decay. And this is the essential justification of the Japanese rule in Korea.

Whether Japan has set herself as a remote aim the training of Korea for self-government I don't know. If she has, she is very optimistic. The Koreans are a delightful people, extremely approachable and full of laughter, but they show not the least aptitude for organized control. They show, indeed, a positive aversion to it, undermining whoever may be in power, whether he be a State official or the pastor of a church, enduring no one to be set over them—in spite of their nationalist gesturing—unless he be a foreigner. And this attitude is not only a negative legacy from centuries of misrule. Chronic bad government is not an inevitable misfortune like a chronic drought. A corrupt and tyrannous Court persisting from generation to generation is a sure sign of national debility. If a people continues to be badly governed it is because they have it in them to be badly governed. Actively or passively they must be held responsible, and not weakly pitied as innocent victims of an evil beyond their power. And the Koreans are such a people. One is tempted to couple with them the Chinese, possibly the Russians, and to formulate a theory that certain races, like certain individuals, are lacking simply in the qualities necessary for rule, just as certain countries may be lacking in the qualities necessary for industry. And in either case such a lack can be made good from outside. Brains for organization can be imported like coal and steel. And not merely brains for organization, but that peculiar gift for judicial rectitude and political honesty which is the portion in some measure of all the Western nations, but in the East of the Japanese alone.

Yet it might be difficult to persuade the Koreans to regard the Japanese merely as a particular kind of import necessary to make good a chance national deficiency. It would be difficult even if you changed the figure, and

suggested that Korea was the employer and
Japan the employee, a business manager, as it
were, for the landed gentleman living at ease on
his estate. And the Japanese might not like it
either. Yet for the life of me I can't see that
imperialism means anything other than that.

We seem to have wandered from Mary Pak.
Her father held a high position under the Korean
Emperor, but, although invited to serve in the
Japanese Government, he refused all office. The
missionaries declared that this was interpreted
as an insult, and that later, when he was thrown
into prison for three years in connection with
some plot against the Governor, it was simply the
Japanese taking a deliberate and spiteful revenge.
Possibly ; possibly not. At any rate my hostess
used to tell me of her visits to the dear man in
prison, enlarging indignantly on his hardships,
clothed as he was summer and winter in a single
thickness of cotton, kept in an unheated cell,
and submitted to a daily baptism of cold water.
But even in prison he contrived to keep a shrewd
eye on the matrimonial affairs of his family, and
did not lose the art of playing the Eastern
despot over his daughter. Yet he was an amusing
old man, entertaining the missionaries with
stories about the Japanese. He was " just that

cute." But as far as I could make out he lived
on the labour of his tenant farmers like any other
landlord, extorting annually his full fifty per
cent. of the produce.

As for Mary, she had many talents. She was
also " just that cute," though where she got
" such notions " from, my hostess even, who
knew her from childhood, couldn't imagine.
She had made a brilliant college career. She was
an admirable debater. She could write choice
English. She could play the violin. Her
teacher, a Czecho-Slovakian and a very excellent
friend of mine, told me that she had " so goot
feeling for the museek and play so naice " but
only " she vill not practees." But I never heard
her perform. She seemed to me to prefer gramophone records of the eukalele and the saxophone.
But she had one unique qualification. She was
a graphologist. She was insatiable in her
demands for hand-writing to be analysed, and her
analyses were astonishing. I forget most of
what she revealed to me about my own character,
but I remember I was logical and sensitive. *So*
sensitive ! So *sensitive !* She gave me to believe
that she had never met any one else quite so
superlatively sensitive. I didn't know whether
to feel flattered or rebuked. But, being logical,
she couldn't understand my obtuseness in not

seeing through the pretences of convention ; and, being sensitive, she couldn't understand my passive acceptance of its tyranny. I was born to be a rebel, but I was a slave.

Yes, in her presence I was a slave. Possibly because I rebelled against her rebellion. Yet away from her I found myself mocking in a manner humiliatingly reminiscent of her own. But with this difference : that being detached from her peculiar perplexities my logic obliged me to include her in my mockery, though being sensitive I sympathized with her with all my heart.

It's a cursed combination, you will find.

But her graphology stood her in good stead. She is analysing hand-writing for an Anglo-Eastern paper. She wrote to me when she received the commission.

" Now I command the attention," she said, " of the great British public."

She seemed hilarious with her success. Her fortune was assured.

Well, she has at least achieved independence. For instance, she needn't kneel to her father on New Year's Day and knock her head three times upon the floor. And for a Korean girl that is emancipation beyond the flight of dreams.

BEYOND THE CITY

XIII

SPORTS OLD AND NEW

THE month was May, as deserving of poetic tribute in Korea as in England. I was with a party of friends, supposedly on a visit to a temple. But we had no one with us of any authority, consequently the temple had little significance for us. I am hazy to this day to which particular deity it was dedicated, though judging by the ferocious images within, and the drums and gongs and weapons and armour, he seemed to be some Oriental Mars. But only a vagueness of memory remains of the shadowy hall and its grim guardians. What I do remember is, in the courtyard outside, a really enormous swing.

It was so lofty a structure that one might well have hesitated before embarking upon it. Also it swayed ominously like the mast of a ship at sea. But the Koreans didn't hesitate. They stood about it in a mass eagerly awaiting their turns. And they made full use of its height, so that one was left speculating on each downward sweep whether the rider would successfully steer between the posts. Not children only, but grown women and grown men. Clearly they were celebrating some sort of a holiday.

But the curious thing was that this was the first swing I had seen in Korea. Yet that same day I saw many others, in the city, on the hills. They seemed to have sprung up like some growth of the night. And in a few days they had vanished again, leaving no trace. Nor did I see another till the following May.

In the same way other sports made sudden transitory appearances. For a day or two in August the boys flew kites. In February they whipped tops, and the girls leapt on see-saws. One saw black, pig-tailed heads bobbing up and down above the walls of courtyards. Or from rising ground one could command a complete view. Quite an astonishing performance. The girls did not sit as in England, but stood, springing high in the air with each upward lift of the plank ; a miracle of balance. And the babies everlastingly strapped to their backs seemed to be no encumbrance.

And in a few days, kites, tops, see-saws, vanished like the swings.

The Oriental mind is insect-like in its instinctive adherence to custom. Presumably

these sports once had some seasonal significance, and in consequence they appear only at the times prescribed. Yet there seems no reason why they should not flourish throughout the year. Perhaps the most amazing thing is the docility with which the children seem to consent to such transitory indulgences. It would be difficult to persuade an English boy to limit his kite-flying or his top-spinning to some three or four days in the year, or a girl to set her dolls, in the manner of the Japanese, in an annual display on shelves to be admired from a distance and packed again in their boxes till the next May festival. But the Easterner's life is ordered, even to children's toys, by ancient codes.

This produces an effect of circumscription and monotony intolerable to the Western mind. Particularly in Korea, where the people entirely lack the Chinese inventiveness and the Japanese fancy. There are no embroideries on the prescribed cut of their customs. As an example, I remember as a boy in China being delighted, sometimes even awed, by the wonderful shapes of the kites : stars and butterflies, hawks and dragons. But in Korea there was only a single pattern : a perfectly unintriguing rectangle, of no size, of no presence, flimsily constructed of split cane and paper, with a circular hole in the centre. And when the festival was over the telegraph wires were ragged with their corpses as though from the tattered relics of some holiday decoration.

For the greater part of the year, I soon discovered, the children were denied their more exciting pastimes. Yet they amused themselves ; the boys with tossing coins, the girls with hopscotch. And there was always the mud of the sewers.

But the schools have adopted the games of the West : base-ball, association football, tennis and general athletics. A lawn is an impossibility in Korea owing to the heavy summer rains and the dryness of the rest of the year, so tennis is played on hard courts only. This should make a fast game ; but the Korean pocket cannot afford the luxury of our club tennis balls, so only soft rubber balls are used. One might add that the customary racket would serve better for lacrosse than for tennis. The result is that the players stand at the far ends of the court and smite the ball to one another with all their might, an " outside " being something in the nature of a feat of strength. Back-handed play is also a rarity, as there is always ample time to change the racket from one hand to the other while awaiting the leisurely approach of the ball. The game is not exactly what we mean by tennis.

Football is played quite well, the Koreans being sturdy and dexterous on their feet. Of base-ball I am not qualified to judge. Yet I used to watch the games. When a match was pending the students would always inform me in their customary manner by writing a notice on the blackboard. On entering the classroom I would find some such information awaiting me : " Dear teacher, to-day great game play with Keiki Commercial School. We hope sincere glorious conquest. You please to come, very kind spare busy time, thank you." And after the match : " Dear teacher, very kind came see unworthy play on so hot day. Alas, we fail, so great shame we like not look you in face. Now we vow terrible revenge."

The particular feature of these contests was the intense seriousness of the onlookers. In Old Japan, I have read somewhere, after a football display by the court players—in full regalia, of course, and with a ball " nine-tenths " filled with air—the captain of the winning team was richly rewarded, and the captain of the losing team soundly flogged. That precise practice has not been carried over to Western football, but something of the spirit remains. There was a really excellent stadium in Keijo, with tennis courts and base-ball ground attached, where the entire schools of the opposing sides sat facing each other in mass. Some half-dozen of the wilder spirits, always conspicuous by their torn uniforms and long hair, constituted themselves leaders of the cheering. They carried flags on long sticks, and at every exciting moment of the game they would leap to the front, vigorously wave their flags in unison—so vigorously that it set their bodies in a grotesque capering to maintain their balance—and howl out a verse of the school song, which the rest accompanied, springing to their feet to do so, and flourishing time with their caps. This was not merely to celebrate success, but to deride ill play on the part of the opponents. In fact, derision was more frequent than applause ; and opponents were never applauded. It all seemed abominably unsporting, until one realized the state of mind both of the players and the spectators. Victory was a vital matter, as though the contest were a battle. And after the game the victorious side would parade the streets of the city, leaning on one another's necks like wounded soldiers, preceded by banner-bearers and followed by the whole school.

My students frequently used to ask me to tell them of games in England. Perhaps I used to exaggerate both the cleanness of our play and the sportingness of our crowds ; but I thought it was good that these people should know that it was part of the game to applaud good play on either side, and at least to refrain from booing. But such practices were completely beyond their range of conception. They must win ; at all costs they must win ; or they were for ever shamed. And to join in dinner with a team by whom they had just been beaten . . . One of the teachers once complained to me about our Western games. These had been introduced into the Eastern schools, he told me, because it had been said that they fostered good fellowship ; but instead of fostering good fellowship they only set the schools at feud with each other. I believed him.

There is no cricket in Korea. The ground would not permit it, apart from its being completely foreign to the genius of the people. Rugby football has just been started. But again I think both the ground and the people will prevent its success. A very excellent and very English friend of mine once wrote to me, " Teach the beggars to play rugger," as though in that game of games lay the panacea for all brooding moods and ugly tempers. But when a game is played in the spirit of warfare Rugby offers too dangerous opportunities for the outlet of hot blood, literally as well as metaphorically. It would keep both the doctors and the police too busy.

The Athletic Meeting—in England we say " Sports' Day "—was a great annual event. It filled the whole day ; contest upon contest, race upon race. Yet it was worth the tedium. It inevitably took place on a Sunday, and the Saturday was a holiday to prepare for it and the Monday a holiday to recover from it. So one was at least one day to the good. Shelters were erected all round the ground, and were thronged with the innumerable visitors who in true Oriental style seemed delighted to sit for hours and watch a monotony of unexciting repetitions. They brought lunches of rice and pickles in little boxes and baskets of fruit, and were in a heaven of contentment. There was a band ; but that was no great attraction. It consisted of fifes and drums with an odd bugle or two, and during the whole day played only one tune. Not between events, as one might have expected, to fill the weary intervals with a light distraction ; but during events. That is, the starting pistol set both racers and band in simultaneous action, and the music stopped as the winner breasted the tape. Stopped not exactly abruptly, but in a ragged succession of instruments,

leaving, as it were, a frayed edge of sound upon
the air.   The Director, in evening dress, sat at a
table piled high with prizes.   Not medals and
silver cups, but pen-holders and pencils and
exercise-books.   The winners received their
rewards after each race, and the idea seemed to
be that everybody must receive some sort of
token.   So medals and cups were hardly to be
expected.

However, there were many amusing events.
One I remember in particular.   The competitors
raced to a point where they received a paper.
The paper bore on it the name of some article
they must borrow from the crowd and carry to
the winning-post.   The spectators were eager
to lend, because the lender of the winning article
also received a prize.   Consequently fountain-
pens and watches and even money were
generously on offer.   But it was an unexpected
diversion to see one of the runners snatch a baby
from its mother and set off for the goal, followed
by the mother, not quite understanding the
motive of the race, in screaming pursuit.   I was
enjoying this refreshing interlude when my friend
the German teacher, who was sitting beside me,
was suddenly seized by the wrist, dragged through
a barricade of chairs, and violently raced round
the track, being another " article."   Well, I was

M

enjoying that too, when I was seized. . . . However, I received a tablet of soap in consolation. . . . And then there was an event for the teachers. A tin was set in the middle of the field. We were blindfolded, and provided with a big stick. Our duty was to march up to the tin and smite it. One or two succeeded. I didn't. But we all received prizes. . . . Apart from the ordinary events there was discus and javelin throwing. Moderately interesting. And a tug-of-war concluded the day. Not a tug-of-war of picked teams, but engaged in, seemingly, by the whole school. There must have been at least a hundred students on each side, and the rope reached from end to end of the field. But of course nothing happened. At each heave the rope seemed to stretch a little, that was all ; so that the rear tuggers of both teams must have thought themselves winning. And the fifes and the drums and the bugles maintained their single tune. And when the affair had continued long enough it was abandoned.

Like this chapter.

A KOREAN GARDEN

XIV

THE AMERICAN MISSIONS

ONCE my hostess and I quarrelled. It was my hostess who apologized, which meant that it was I who was to blame. I admit it. I was deliberately provocative. Without exactly intending to chafe her into open anger, I yet wished to annoy ; more, I wished to hurt ; and seemingly I succeeded. But it was very impertinent of me, because the matter in question was no affair of mine. Yet it was one of those matters on which we all feel at liberty to speak. Because there was a savour of hypocrisy in it, always a public butt for criticism. Expressed in the abstract it was the contrast between profession and practice. Expressed in the concrete—— But it came about like this.

My hostess was boasting—at least, I considered she was boasting—of the comforts, advantages and emoluments of the missionary life. That may sound incredible to you, because at the " home base " one hears only of the hardships and the hazards. But on the " field "—I refer exclusively to Korea, not being qualified to speak of other countries—it would be difficult, among the American missions, to supply evidence of these hardships and hazards. Indeed, between themselves the missionaries make a joke of these fund-provoking yarns. Let me quote a Methodist bishop—for the American Methodists have bishops, you must know.

" When people at home ask me," I heard him say at a dinner-party, " however the missionaries manage to exist, I always want to answer, ' My good people, the missionaries have everything that you have, and a lot more besides.' "

And the missionaries laughed, appreciating, I suppose, the humour of their deception, and realizing that the dinner-party itself was a proof of the truth of the bishop's remark. And as a further example : a missionary refugee from China after the 1927 upheaval told us with delicious candour that the first time the bishop came to visit her she put away her Peking rugs and her best furniture because she thought it might give a wrong impression.

" But," she continued, " when he saw my bare floors he burst out laughing and said, ' You needn't hide your rugs from me. I know how missionaries live.' "

It was such a relief, she told us. He was such

an understanding man. . . . Well, when my
hostess began to enlarge on her husband's ample
salary, on their comfortable house, on the
excellent education they had provided for their
children, and the excellent marriages their
children had made, on the presents showered on
them annually by friends at home, on the choice
of houses and automobiles that seemed to await
them on retirement in America, as well as the
little item of a generous pension, I remembered
those two stories which I have just told you, and
a train of other circumstances, besides, of which
they were but acute illustrations, and I felt in
the ironical part of me a challenge to conflict.
I said I wished I had known all that before,
because I should have become a missionary
myself, as it seemed a most paying profession.
And after that we quarrelled.

All this is not so trivial as it may seem. What
strikes the outsider at the very commencement is
the almost luxurious style in which the missionaries live. And not only the outsider. The new
missionaries fresh from home, where they have
been expectantly bracing themselves to a life
of cramping sacrifices, look on at first in dismay.
As a young Canadian expressed it to me, not
without bitterness :

" I got through college without once needing

a dress-suit, but now that I've come to the mission field I must either buy a dress-suit or refuse half my invitations to dinner."

But more important than the effect on the outsider, or on the new missionary, is the effect on the native ; which justifies one in choosing such a starting-point in a consideration of missions.

To the ordinary native, then, Christianity quite obviously is hardly distinguishable from Westernism. It means large brick houses, servants, social prestige—in short, amplitude and prosperity as opposed to mean degradation. An amplitude and prosperity to be attained through education, hence the natives flock to the mission schools ; as the wiser, or bolder, missionaries will confess. You may take as witness of this the students at the Methodist seminary in the compound where I lodged. These students, presumably, were the pick of the Korean Christians, as they were definitely preparing for the native ministry. Their syllabus included some eight periods a week of English. It was suggested that this was a complete waste of time, as no village pastor in Korea would find any use for English, and accordingly it was proposed to abolish English from the syllabus. Promptly the students went on strike, threatening to leave in a body unless English were reinstated.

The significance was unmistakable. To the Korean—to the Japanese too—English, rightly or wrongly, is the open sesame to any successful career. To such an extent that one is pestered everywhere, in trams, in trains, by progressive young men anxious to learn English. " Please will you teach me English ? " they accost you, so that you feel inclined to answer, " Certainly ; if you can spare a few minutes I'll teach you now." Though actually you put them off by mention of a fee. To counter this the more subtle ones will ask you to teach them " Bibble," assuming that religious instruction will gladly be given free. But you can unmask the motive quite simply by recommending them to some missionary, at which they will shake their heads and say, " But he teach Korean Bibble. I wish to read Bibble in English." You see the point. These theological students who threatened to leave the seminary if English teaching were denied them had no intention of remaining village pastors all their days. It was my host himself— one of the most genuine, patient and laborious missionaries I have ever met—who confessed to me that all these men wanted was to take advantage of the mission education to qualify themselves for commercial appointments. Not, I think, that they were more unscrupulous than their fellows, but simply because the missionaries have failed to distinguish for them Christianity and Western materialistic progress.

Yet one can sympathize with the missionary and appreciate his problem. It is a truism to say that it's useless to preach to a man with an empty stomach. It's equally useless to preach to a whole people sunk in a degrading poverty. The early missionary was driven to include a certain materialistic uplift as an essential in his creed. He was obliged to preach better food, better clothes, better houses, as well as the salvation of the soul, because without these things the soul showed no symptoms of salvation. But to preach these things implied education. And there the trouble began. Instead of being satisfied with an education adapted to the simple needs of Korea, the missions imported Western education intact, with its elaborate equipment and expensive buildings. But the scholars didn't attend the missionary schools because they wanted to become Christians. It was absurd to suppose that they would. They saw in them merely the road to individual advancement, and they patronized them accordingly.

This is clear to-day from the frequent school strikes, as much a feature of the mission schools as the Government schools. The Chosen

Christian College was on strike when I left Korea. It began, I believe, in the commercial department. Certain demands were made, but were rejected by the authorities. Consequently the whole department went on strike. The authorities countered by issuing an ultimatum that all students who failed to return to classes by a certain day would be automatically expelled from the College. Some returned ; and those who didn't were accordingly declared to be expelled. This occasioned a further strike among those who had returned, demanding the reinstatement of their fellows, which was refused. The following night the College was surrounded by the strikers who sat wailing on the hills.

"How can we rejoice any more," they lamented, " when our brothers are dead ? "

As a result, the complete commercial department was obliterated. As a further result the whole College threatened to join in a sympathetic strike. That was the situation when I left. Not an isolated case, mind you, but a periodic occurrence in every school. The significance is that the students consider that the missionaries are there, not to teach them what the missionaries think fit, but to teach them what they themselves want to learn ; that is, such things as will qualify them to compete in the business market. And they are justified, since the missionaries include science, medicine and commerce, in their syllabus.

There is a tendency to break from this now and leave education to the Japanese Government. But I can't help thinking that the missions are afraid of such a step. To some extent it would be an admission, perhaps not of failure, but at least of grave misjudgment. Also there would be a difficulty with the individual missionary, a man of different calibre from the pioneer missionary of the last two generations. To return to almost purely evangelical work would mean to return to the primitive conditions of some thirty years ago when the missionaries lived among the people, in native houses, perhaps eating native food and wearing native clothes. But to-day this is not simply not practised, it is definitely discountenanced. The new recruits clamour for permission to make the experiment; but they are severely discouraged, being threatened with every imaginable disease, culminating in insanity. They owe it to their work, they are told, to take a rightful care of their health, which can only be done by living in sanitary Western houses and eating digestible Western food. Yet one or two persist, and spend an occasional month in the country living in Korean style; but they rapidly come under the

spell of their commodious homes, and, easy
converts to the creed of " rightful care of health,"
themselves indoctrinate the new-comers. There
was, however, when I left Korea, one bold rebel
who had adopted Korean dress and wore it
even in the capital. Yet he wasn't of the bold,
rebellious type. He was a particularly meek
sort of fellow, soft-spoken, and given to playing
sentimental hymn tunes. One wondered why
he had come abroad without his mother.
Indeed, when I heard it stated that he would do
well to be married, I couldn't resist the suggestion
that he would make a sweet wife if the girl were
a kind husband. And yet he had the courage to
stand alone against the formidable disapproval
of all his colleagues. A disapproval whose
peculiar acrimony betrayed its real motive. It
was perfectly clear that the older missionaries
felt themselves rebuked by this upstart. His
adoption of Korean dress was a definite condemnation of their own Western clothes. And
that they should feel it as a condemnation was a
revelation of uneasy consciences. Because the
matter didn't end with a question of trousers
versus pantaloons. It opened that wider
question, on which the modern missionary is
very touchy, namely : effectively to preach the
Gospel to a primitive people, how far must a

man conform to the conditions of that people, and how far may he indulge himself in the amenities of the civilization to which he is accustomed? Quite frankly, the Korean missionary has no convincing answer, because he has set his line of indulgence so high. For instance, even the " rightful care of health " theory hardly justifies a house which demands four servants to its upkeep and a consumption of twenty-four tons of coal a year. This is so entirely out of proportion with the beggarly standard of the country ; and it is because he knows this that the Korean missionary is so readily stirred to anger by the unsolicited criticisms of outsiders, particularly of impertinent outsiders like myself who suggest that the missionary's is a paying profession. However, although it was impertinent of me, yet I was glad I angered my hostess ; because her anger, in the particular form in which it expressed itself, assured me of what I already suspected : that the missionaries are conscious themselves of something not entirely apostolic in their adopted level of living. And it is this very standard which will make it extremely difficult for them to revert from their elaborate educational policy to the evangelical policy of earlier days. Yet, if they do not revert, their work will increasingly become, not a mere negative waste, but a positive menace, by fostering that most detestable of all Eastern types—the man who through a smattering of Western learning has come to despise his own people.

It's very sad, but that seems to me the fruit of missionary education in Korea. An example will show that the missionaries are not altogether blameless. One dear man—this was at another dinner-party—related with fervent pride how he received an unexpected contribution for his church. It came from a family of farmers. It was a gift of gratitude. It happened like this. The missionary in his travels had evidently met these farmers whom he found in a poor way. They explained their poverty by the low price they received for their rice. The missionary suggested the simple expedient of storing the rice until the winter and selling when the price rose. This had never occurred to these innocent people. However, they followed the advice, built barns, kept their rice till prices were high, and sold at a big profit. In gratitude, although not Christians, they made a handsome contribution to the missionary's church. And the missionary was delighted. He had persuaded the unprovident Koreans to be provident. If only he could persuade all the Koreans to be equally provident, in a very short time they would become a prosperous nation. That was how he argued, this very simple man who had felt himself elected of the Holy Spirit to preach the Gospel of Christ to the heathen in their darkness. But when I asked him how the matter must appear to the poor folk who had to buy the rice at a higher figure, he seemed not to have considered their point of view. And I didn't press with the further question as to what would happen if everybody stored their rice waiting for the prices to rise. Nor did I suggest, though it was in my mind, that it would be more illustrative of his Gospel if he could provide practical examples of how *not* to take advantage of one's neighbours. So, to come back in a circle, you see how very easy it must be for the Koreans to confuse Christianity with Western progress.

As for my hostess, it was very wrong of me to provoke that quarrel. For after all she had spent nearly forty years in Korea. She had served her term in the front line, and had endured harrowing sorrows. But then, people can't be allowed to have it both ways. If they are to be honoured for their sacrifices they mustn't vaunt their salaries and their mansions and their automobiles.

However, as I haven't yet apologized let me apologize now.

XV

THE ENGLISH FATHERS

THOUGH no churchman, I was always welcomed by the Fathers of the English Church. It's difficult to say precisely what drew me to them, yet I was continually dropping in for tea and gossip. The simple fact was that I liked them. I liked their English manner, their English speech. I liked the casual homeliness of their common-room, with English papers scattered on the arms of chairs, and its English fire. Also I liked their English cake. And there was the further item that one was permitted to smoke. Because the American missionaries looked on smoking as something damnable, like drunkenness or debauchery; consequently I could never season an after-dinner cup of coffee with a cigarette or a cigar, but must retire to my room and indulge my vice in solitude; or if held by company downstairs I must appease my nerves with the lulling comforts of a rocker. And I always felt that the conversation about me owed its blatant puerility to the

lack of the mellowing fragrance of tobacco.
But the English Fathers were so astonishingly
human. So human that one forgot entirely
that they robed themselves in cassocks and
belted themselves with cords. Simply, one was
at ease.

If I introduce them to you by their real names
and without disguise it will not be taken, I hope,
as a betrayal of friendship, but rather, as I
intend it, as an acknowledgment that they were
so thoroughly worth knowing. Yet it is difficult
to find terms to describe them. To say
" educated " or " of good family," or to be more
precise and say " of the Public School and
Varsity type," is inadequate. One must add
that they were the sort of well-bred men who
bear their breeding as an athlete bears his
strength, unselfconsciously and without flourish.
And yet, of course, what one noticed were the
oddities that individualized them, which you
might say detached them humanly from that
serene background. And what one did not
notice was that they were churchmen, though I
should imagine this must have been the supreme
distinction of which they themselves were aware.

Perhaps Father Hunt was more obviously a
churchman than the rest, but only in company,
and particularly in the company of ladies. On

these occasions—for instance, when lecturing on old English carols to the Music Club—he had the delicious manner of the curate to whom the female sex are " sweet things " to be amused and cajoled. To heighten this you must remember that most of the " sweet things " in Keijo were American to whom both English humour and English speech—particularly of the Oxford variety—were equally incomprehensible. To them such performances were of the nature of comic parody, Father Hunt, all unconsciously to himself, appearing to them as an exact replica of the Englishman on the American stage. And they flocked to hear him, admitting that they didn't understand half of what he said, but finding him " so entertaining." It was very jolly.

Father Hunt was growing corpulent, but Father Drake—we were not related—was tall and thin. An elderly man, who would have struck one as a severe ascetic, as possibly he was, if his eyes had not been in a perpetual twinkle and his lips constantly a-twitch for a smile. He had his humour too, the more delightful for the astonishing softness of his voice. Once my hostess asked him to sing—Father Hunt sang well in a rich baritone. He declined, but admitted that once he had thought of taking lessons.

N

" But you know," he told us with an air of
gentle confession, " when I tried to show what
I could do my teacher stopped me. ' You
positively mustn't,' he said. ' It's dreadful,
dreadful ! I can't endure it ! ' "

He read Byron. Father Hunt preferred
Michael Arlen. Father Drake had once em-
barked on a Michael Arlen. It was reported to
me that after perusing a page or two he closed
the book with a snap and issued the stern
command :

" Take this dung away."

His comment to me was that as he found
adultery on the first page he didn't dare imagine
what there might be on the last. At which
Father Hunt protested :

" But it was *clean* adultery," and offered to lend
me the book so that I might judge between them.

These people were celibates, which made
their tea-parties amusing, as they were in the
habit of reaching for what they required in the
manner of bachelors, and left their guests to
reach in the same way. Bishop Trollope poured
out the tea—incidentally they had taught their
servant how to make tea, an accomplishment
unknown to the servants of the Americans,
though in compensation they had learnt how to
make coffee. His lordship was a powerfully

built man with an intellect to match his girth. Not satisfied with the mere mastery of Korean, he must study Japanese and Chinese as well. But for all his scholarship there was no dryness in his conversation. He was so alertly interested in everything that in his company talk never flagged; to such an extent that one must admit that he forgot his duties as host. Imposingly arrayed in purple cassock, he would brandish the teapot, all unmindful of the necessity of pouring out tea, while he discoursed on Homer and Japanese education and the novels of his name-sake. When Father Hunt gently reminded him that his guests were thirsty he would pour out the tea indeed, but would leave the cups standing at his elbow while be broached fresh topics of conversation. I have one picture of him in my mind, holding a returned cup high in air, and looking rather helplessly about the tea-table.

"We don't appear to have a slop-pail," he announced at length. He realized he had used a wrong term, and looking at Father Hunt in a puzzled way said, "I don't think that's quite right, is it?"

"No, my lord," Father Hunt replied with an air of respectful correction, "we call it a slop-*basin*. A slop-*pail* is a thing we keep in a bedroom."

Celibacy was no mere incidental trifle to the English Fathers. It was a policy definitely adopted and insisted on by the bishop, not, I think, in the manner of the Roman Church as being a sign of the sanctification of the priesthood, but because it simplified and intensified the missionary's work in the foreign field. As it does. It definitely distinguishes the Anglican Church from the Nonconformist churches in Korea, which, as it happens, with the exception of the Salvation Army, are American or Canadian. Distinguishes, that is, not so much the men, as the type of service they can offer. It carries with it as an immediate result lower salaries, which means more missionaries to the funds available. It means, too, smaller houses. The large houses of the Nonconformist missionaries are the corollary of wives and children ; particularly when you remember that the missionary's wife is not necessarily a missionary, and so demands the home comforts to which she has been accustomed ; demands, too, full amenities for social intercourse, her one occupation, having none of the duties and amusements of the West. But for the unmarried man a large house would be an encumbrance. Indeed, the English Fathers in the capital live communally. Quartered in the Cathedral com-

pound, they share a very modest block of single-
story native buildings, adapted and furnished,
of course, to their needs. They live with
astonishing frugality, heroically circumscribing
themselves within the limits of bare comfort—
if that even. Father Hunt's study, for example,
furnished with a small reading-table and chair
at one end, a stand set with crucifix and candles
at the other, and bookshelves at one side,
hardly admits of a couple of further chairs—
imported from the bedroom next door—for
visitors ; while the bedroom with narrow bed
and washstand is even more crampingly confined.
But for a celibate this suffices.

The celibate, too, can give undistracted
attention to his work. Quite apart from the
extra time at his disposal, he can expose himself
to risks without worrying about the possible
consequences to wife and children. He can
mix freely with all men in all places. He is
mobile. But life is not easy for him. He
suffers at times from an intolerable loneliness.
To such an extent that the married missionary
likes to tell you, though basing his generalization
on very meagre evidence, that the celibate goes
mad ; which may account for the married
missionary's startling proneness to second and
third marriages, purely in self-defence, one may

suppose, against insanity. And it is noteworthy that it is the married missionary who criticises the celibate, not, as one might suppose, the celibate who criticises the married man. Criticises him with distinct acrimony, and rejoices when, as sometimes happens, he succumbs to a wife, and consequently withdraws to another field. Yet these particular celibates showed no visible symptoms of incipient insanity. On the contrary, they seemed particularly stable and assured, not even inclining to the freakish.

The Church Mission, apart from the question of celibacy, stands in sharp contrast with the Nonconformist missions in its methods of service. Its aim is concentration as opposed to expansion. It does not organize vast schools, but maintains modest hostels, the hostel in the capital, included in the Cathedral compound, housing some thirty boys only. But the boys are specially chosen, and are under constant supervision. The influence brought to bear on them is not educational—they attend such schools as they wish—but, you might say, paternal. It is the influence of the home. The underlying idea is that to produce a few staunch Christians and send them out among their fellows to be centres of further influence is more effective than an indiscriminate mass instruction where the

individual is lost in the community. Logically
the principle seems sound, though whether it is
justified in the practice I don't know. The
English Fathers seemed as pessimistic of their
results as the Nonconformist missionaries. I
have heard Father Drake say, with an air of
pained disgust, that quite half the hostel boys
were living immoral lives ; and Father Hunt
seemed to return from his visits to country
churches in increasing despondency, complaining
that the Koreans were mere blocks of wood
entirely unresponsive to any spiritual appeal ;
which I think is the secret of the failure of
missions in Korea. The people are simply not
of the stuff of which Christians are made, just
as they are not of the stuff of which rulers are
made. Heaven has created them so.

The Cathedral itself is a beautiful granite
building, Byzantine in style. It is not yet
complete, lacking transepts, and still to be
extended to half again of its present length.
Yet, even so, it stands up resolute and serene
against the blue Korean sky. It is white within,
giving it an air of clean spaciousness. The choir
is faced with Irish marble, and the alcove behind
the altar has recently been inlaid with mosaic.
Its mere size is significant when you consider
that its congregation consists of little more than

the thirty boys from the hostel and perhaps as many girls from the convent. Especially when you contrast it, say, with the chapel at the Chosen Christian College, which, built for some hundreds of students, is yet a mere elongated attic at the top of one of the buildings, with a desk for a pulpit, and a photograph of the founder for the image of Christ. This symbolizes for you the vital difference not only in method but in outlook of the Anglican and the Nonconformist missions. Central and dominant in the one is the Cathedral, built less for the present than for futurity. Central and dominant in the other are the lecture-halls and the laboratories, with the place of worship relegated to an obscure corner as though admitted only on sufferance. Standing outside them both I don't pretend to judge between them. I merely note the contrast with its implied interpretation ; but which is the superior, or whether the two are complementary, each expressing an equally valid attitude, I can't pretend to say.

Father Hunt was something of a connoisseur of Korean art. He used to bargain occasionally for a picture or a screen. He used to display these very faded productions to me, attempting with head to one side and soft gestures of the hands to make me appreciate their beauties.

I'm afraid I was very hypocritical, pretending
to appreciate when for the life of me I saw no
beauty at all. I accompanied him, too, to
museums and temples. Some of the old pottery
I did admire, and the temples I always enjoyed.
I should have enjoyed them more if I could have
followed the conversations between Father Hunt
and the priests. Yet even these, unintelligible
as they were, were amusing as pantomime. The
bowing and the folding of hands were eloquent
of the mutual forbearance of antagonists too
polite to come to an open breach. And Father
Hunt's exaggerated gutturals gave me the impression that he spoke Korean even with an
Oxford accent. But his attitude to Buddhism
pleased me. Not only would he remove his
hat in the temples and speak with subdued
voice, but he was capable of a sincere respect
for the teachings of Buddha and a genuine delight
in the symbolism of the images, which less
sympathetic missionaries are apt to dismiss as
heathenism and idolatry. But the dear man
was growing corpulent, as I have told you ; and
as our excursions invariably took place on
scorching days, and as the hills were steep, he
would fan himself with a vigorous pertinacity,
exclaiming from time to time, " Really, you
know, I find this weather most trying." His

servant would follow us with an immense lunch basket, complete with kettle and teapot. I was his guest, and he refreshed me well.

On one occasion we lunched in a temple of peculiar interest. Above the temple itself was a shrine built out upon a platform levelled on the mountain-side. Within was a picture of an old man with a tiger-cat nestling at his feet. The priest explained that this was the Spirit of the Mountain, which led to a discourse on the way in which Buddhism had become overlaid with primitive animistic beliefs. For the same priest tended both the altar of Buddha and the shrine of the Mountain Spirit. Later I was to find that this was universal in Korea. All the temples were decorated with beasts actual or legendary, representing natural forces at first hostile to Buddhism but later adopted and incorporated in its worship so that one could not tell which was the conqueror and which was the conquered. In the Diamond Mountains, indeed, every peak and every pool has its legend of the conflict between the Buddhas and the creatures of the waters and the rocks. But that is another story. Father Hunt the idealist deplored the intrusion of that old man and the cat, being as solicitous for a pure Buddhism as for a pure Christian Church.

TEMPLE PAINTING:
"THE SPIRIT OF THE MOUNTAIN"

That was a moment of insight for me, and by the light of it I was able to understand what one of the other Fathers meant when he told me that it would not distress him if all the churches in Korea were abandoned ; he would be quite willing to remain and perform services in the empty Cathedral, would prefer the empty Cathedral, in fact, to its present congregations. And here I will venture an opinion. To go out into the highways and the byways and compel people to enter may be in accordance with the letter of the Scriptures, but it will never make for a powerful Church.

But then I speak without authority.

XVI

FATHER CALISTUS

I HAD reasons for wishing to visit the north of Korea. When it came to the point, however, in my last Easter vacation, I found I only had four days at my disposal. As the journey each way would consume twenty-four hours, I should have exactly two days for my visit. But distances in the East are of no account. A three-hours' train journey preliminary to a day's hike was an almost weekly occurrence. And when my wife joined me out East it seemed perfectly fitting that I should go to Tokyo—forty-eight hours by land and sea— to meet her. Like dropping over to Warsaw or down to Rome, for instance, to meet a friend returning West. And this particular case might be comparable to a Londoner's spending a week-end in the north of Scotland. If such a proposal were made to him you might at least expect him to temporize. But it simply didn't occur to me to temporize. The only question was, where best to put up. Because to stay at

an inn would not be very profitable, as I could
not expect to learn much if left entirely to my
own observations. I needed some one who knew
the country, who knew the people, and who
would be able to put me rapidly in touch with
the conditions there. I found such a man in
Father Calistus.

Father Calistus ! The name is no invention
of my own. I find it so enchanting that I
cannot bring myself to pervert it with some
literary disguise. Nor does the man need any
mask. And I can offer him no higher tribute
of my regard than to draw for you his portrait
with an unscrupulous fidelity.

He lived in the frontier town of Kwainei on
the Tuman River, which on the north-east
marks the border between Manchuria and Korea.
Precisely the spot I wished to see. There was
a Canadian Mission there where I should
undoubtedly have been welcomed, but I had
heard so much of the hospitality of the Roman
Church, and it promised also a new experience
and a new outlook, that on receiving the name
of Father Calistus from a friend of mine in Keijo
I wrote to him to ask if he could accommodate
me. Incidentally I was honest enough to tell
him that I was a novelist and that my curiosity
was purely professional. This seemingly did not

disturb him—possibly he had had no acquaintance with our breed—for he replied at once with an unqualified invitation, warning me only that he had little English—he belonged to the German Mission—and bidding me " clothe me warmly " as it was still very cold in the north. I obeyed.

I arrived at Kwainei in the morning. The journey of the previous day had been romantic enough, the line running by a coast of bluffs and bays fringed rockily with islands. But with the morning we left the sea, turning inland among shrubby hills, increasingly bleak and desolate, with snow lying on the higher summits. Father Calistus met me at the station. One picked him out at a glance. Bearded, goggled, muffled in long, black cloak and cape, with face framed within the cheek-pieces of his sheepskin hat, in one hand a stout staff, he was the complete picture of the Roman priest. He greeted me pleasantly but without gush, which established between us at once a friendly, matter-of-fact relationship. He eyed my rucksack, my sole kit. It was simpler to let me carry it myself without fuss than to put me to the awkwardness of an expostulation by offering to carry it for me. I was grateful to him. He led me to his house.

I was a little surprised, and at first disappointed, because somehow I had got it into

my head that Father Calistus was a monk and
that I was to be lodged at a monastery, having
in mind other monasteries, at Keijo, Gensan and
elsewhere.   But there was no monastery.   Father
Calistus lived entirely alone, except for his
Korean "boy," in a native-style house in a
rather mean alley off the main street of the
town.   In fact, he lived completely native, except
for his dress and a minimum of furniture.   His
house consisted of two rooms, with a vestibule—
possibly two yards square—by which one entered.
It had the customary platform and low veranda
open to the customary court.   The rooms were
very small and very low.   One was furnished
with a little desk, two straight-backed, unup-
holstered chairs, and a bookcase.   Some prints
of the Virgin and a crucifix or two, and a
German calendar showing a scene of flowering
meadows and blue hills, hung from nails on the
walls.   The other room, entered by a sliding
screen, was, I found later, quite bare except for
a rude washstand.   This was the bedroom, but
there was no bed, Father Calistus sleeping like
the Koreans on a quilt on the floor.   There was
one other room opening from this, the kitchen,
but I have not included it in the apartments of
Father Calistus as it formed the boy's quarters,
though an occasional hint suggested that the

Father himself sometimes lent a hand with the cooking and cleaning. There were no stoves in the house, the floors being heated from beneath. But the floors were meaner than those I had been accustomed to. They were of bare earth, loosely laid over with thin straw mats. Warm enough to the feet, but impossible to keep free of vermin.

We sat in the study-sitting-room for a little and talked, drinking innumerable cups of sugared but milkless tea poured from a kettle. With the two of us in the room there was little space to spare, and none to stretch one's legs at ease. One felt a certain sad confinement, the effect not merely of the narrowly enclosing walls and the low ceiling, but of the meagre light insufficient even for such a mean interior. The single window, papered except for a small square of glass, admitted only a filtered dimness. And through the glass one looked upon an empty courtyard and a blank wall. The place was a prison, a tomb. Yet we drank tea, and we talked. Also we smoked. I discovered quite soon that for Father Calistus his pipe served as wife, as friends, as music, as theatre, as literature. For though there were books on his shelves he told me he was too " laizy " to read. And what was there that he could read which would help him in his relations with these simple people? Their lives consisted of labour, relieved of monotony merely by births, marriages and deaths. Nothing more. Books would not teach him to understand them, nor to sympathize with them. Yet when he was younger he had also studied theology. When he was younger. . . . He sucked vigorously at his pipe to make certain that the last shred of tobacco had been consumed, then tapped it out and refilled it.

" De pipe," he commented, in his broken English, " ees—*wie sagt man?*—de best *Freund.*"

He had been nineteen years in Korea. He had never once returned to Germany. When did he expect to go, I asked him. He shrugged with a gentle patience :

" Perhaps some day ; perhaps never."

I glanced at the calendar with its blue hills and flowering meadows. Korea was a beautiful land, but there were no meadows. After two years I was hankering for fields of buttercups and rich, deep grass, and for hills with gentle outlines. Already the granite summits, wildly pinnacled like arrested flames, were taking on something of the fantastic, something of the monstrous, from which one needed to escape for a little to landscapes suaver, saner. But nineteen years. . . . Yet the pipe is a great

o

consoler. Father Calistus had achieved the
faculty of smoking Korean tobacco, a fine hair-
like weed which catches one at the back of the
throat at the first inhalation, and at the third
brings violently to mind one's youthful experiments with blotting-paper. Its recommendation
was that one could smoke it without cessation
throughout one's whole waking day at an outlay
of three shillings a month, and that in a country
where European tobacco is nearly three times its
price in England. He had also achieved the
faculty of eating Korean food and drinking—
" eet is goot for de—*wie sagt man?*—*Verdauung*"—
Korean brandy. It may have been good for
the digestion, and living without other pre-
cautions, dining as he did with the natives in
their own hovels, it might even have been
necessary ; but I found it rank and repugnant
to the palate. As, indeed, I must confess I
found the messes which his boy concocted for
us at meals : stewed and stringy meats soaked in
ill-savouring sauces, greasy pancakes, sour *kimchi*.
Or if not actually repugnant, at least unappetiz-
ing, unsatisfying, leaving a craving behind for
sweet puddings and fruits. But I hope I betrayed
none of this ; for the food I was obliged to
eat, and the brandy and tobacco I sampled in
moderation from some obscure sense of duty.

And if by any remote possibility Father Calistus should ever come to read this confession I hope he will take it, not as a disparagement of his taste, but as a tribute to his heroism. For at first he must have experienced the same revolt as myself, but he had schooled himself through endurance to an actual relish of the fare. It was part of his mission. Also it was an economic necessity. For I elicited from him a declaration of his resources, being impertinently curious, I admit, to compare him with the Protestant missionaries of the capital. He received a hundred yen (ten pounds) a month, he told me. Living native style it cost him perhaps twenty yen a month to feed himself and his boy, and another twenty yen for clothes. Then tobacco, that was one yen fifty, and one must write letters to one's people.

" So, *wissen Sie*, I can a leetle to the poor give."

He told me this quite simply, with no suggestion that there might be anything meritorious in his sacrifice. Indeed, he seemed rather anxious that I should not overestimate his poverty, adding that friends sent him clothes, and sometimes a tin of milk or even a box of cigars. He had all that was necessary.

During my two days with him he led me about the countryside, showing me whatever seemed to him likely to interest me as an author. We visited a coal mine, an old mountain fortress, the Tuman River, the homes of some of his parishioners.

" But I know not what you seek," he confessed. " In all this there is nothings."

As it happened there was a great deal. The coal mine opened, not by a shaft, but by a tunnel slanting down into the earth. The Japanese manager led us through the galleries, which followed the twisting veins of coal between walls of granite and basalt. We followed, carrying open acetylene lamps. There was no eight-hour day there, we learnt, but two twelve-hour shifts. The workers, Koreans—even in the mine they wore white clothes—looked pale and seedy. They seemed to live in single-roomed houses, where the families swarmed together like rabbits. And always the price of coal increased, Father Calistus told me, and the wages decreased. The improved sanitary conditions had flooded the market with workers. There were always men to be found. And if there were an accident, or if they starved on their little money, what did it matter ? They were only poor Koreans.

The mountain fortress was much the same as others I had seen ; a large space of hills enclosed with a rambling wall, built in the days when the Manchu raiders had swept periodically over the border. The Tuman was still frozen, a wide water, curving between cliffs and shingly beaches, with the bare, fierce mountains of Manchuria looming up beyond. Here and there among the shingle some dead fruit-trees showed where a sudden inundation had devastated farms and orchards. The cottages were deserted. It would be impossible ever to clear away the waste of stones. The people had wandered elsewhere. Perhaps into Manchuria itself. There was no relief. Many must have starved. But what did it matter? They were only poor Koreans.

Yet Father Calistus spoke without bitterness. He had lived so close to this earthy and necessitous people that participation in their piteous calamities had mellowed him to a peculiar patience. It wasn't resignation, it wasn't fortitude. His lips softly pouting through the unrazed growth of his beard, his eyes quietly observant behind his goggles, his little, cloaked, slow-moving figure, unshaken by the gusty wind, untroubled by the icy air, spoke of a gentle endurance in harmony with the sad necessities of an existence which bore implicit in its grievous visitations a solace and a hope. And this was the message which he carried with him. Here and there where the cottagers knew him they came tumbling from their hovels to greet him, stepping into their sandals which lay at their doors, their heads bent to pass beneath the lintels, one upon another like animals from a conjuror's hat, smiling and bowing him salutations as he approached, welcoming him in, setting straw cushions on the floor, trays with fish and *kimchi*, tobacco—they knew his weakness —standing about him, or consenting to squat when he had entreated them to be at ease, garrulously answering his inquiries, while the women and the girls peeped in from the kitchen doorway. He would eat with them, drink with them, smoke with them, was one of them. But what had they to offer him, what of sustaining companionship in his loneliness cut off from his own people without prospect of return? And in his own house it was the same. While we talked together, even at our meals, men, women, little boys, popped in and out of the vestibule, perhaps standing at the door merely to gaze at us, perhaps maintaining endless throaty monologues while we ate or smoked. And there was no escape. Except for one week in the year when he went for a holiday to one or other of the monasteries. I asked him how he endured it. " I have my pipe, *wissen Sie*," he replied.

The real answer, of course, was in the little chapel adjacent to his house where he repaired

morning and evening, and for a few minutes
when we returned from our walks. There he
would kneel on the bare floor, his hands pressed
together, his face towards the altar. An altar
set with candles and gaudy with bright colours,
with the suffering image of Christ only half
visible because of the dividing wall partitioning
the men's side of the chapel from the women's.
Well, he found there what he needed.

At night he took down quilts from a shelf in
the bedroom and himself laid them for me on the
floor, sprinkling around them a protective barricade of powder, " because of de—*wie sagt man ?*—
Wanzen." I undressed by candlelight, careful
to put my clothes on the little rickety washstand
out of contact with the infected walls and floor.
But I contracted no bugs. The memories that
remained to me had nothing of that unpleasantness in them. Yet they were less of what I had
set out to see than of a simple and sacrificial
life which had been unexpectedly revealed to
me, a life without sublimities, but humbly and
patiently heroic.

When I returned to Keijo I could think of no
better expression of my gratitude and esteem
than to send Father Calistus a supply of tobacco
and a box of cigars.

XVII

THE ENGLISH LESSON

IT was a very hot afternoon in July. In three more days the terminal examinations would begin ; a week later, the vacation. I had had no lessons in the morning, so I didn't arrive at the school till after tiffin. The tram, with its shutters drawn against the sun, and the air blowing down it, had been comparatively cool ; but the three-minutes' walk from the terminus, along a dusty road, beneath a blazing sky, left me with garments clammily clinging to thighs and back. I had started from home with the excellent intention of amusing my students— work seeming intolerable on such a day—but by the time I reached the staff room I was in no mood for amusement; the mere prospect of it brought me out in fresh waves of perspiration. To tell a funny story with laborious slowness, to repeat it three times ; then to explain the point with painful exactitude, to repeat that three times ; then to call upon the students one by one to retell the story, only

to become convinced of what one already suspected—that the joke had been hopelessly mis-
understood. . . . All this in an atmosphere of
exuding torpor—impossible. The story must
wait.

Having bowed to the teachers in the staff
room, hung up my sun-helmet, rinsed my hands
and face in the basin by the door, I sat down at
my desk and looked through my papers to see
how I could shift from myself to my pupils the
burden of the " amusement " of the next two
hours.

The " boy-san " brought me a cup of hot tea—
Japanese tea, pale amber in colour, milkless and
sugarless. The cup had no handle. It burnt
my fingers as I took it from the tray. I didn't
drink the tea immediately. I set it down to
cool, and continued to search among my papers.
I found some readings, some notes for conversation ; but these would involve myself too
strenuously. An old examination paper ; the
very thing. Among certain questions in English
there were some five lines of Japanese print. A
business letter, I remembered. I would set the
poor victims to translate that.

I had a few minutes to spare. There were a
couple of Japanese teachers of English who had
difficulties to consult me about. One was

reading Galsworthy's " Justice " with his students, the other Hardy's " Life's Little Ironies." I explained the perplexing passages, realizing that English slang—or popular idiom, shall we say?—and English grammatical construction, must contain many elements of obscurity for logical Eastern minds.

Another teacher approached me, energetically fanning himself, bowing jerkily from the hips with every second step forward, and smiling with an irresistible amiability. His front teeth were framed in gold.

" *Saa !* " he exclaimed somewhat throatily, " veree hot weathah, yess ? Veree hot for you, I think. Veree in-con-ven-yent."

He had said exactly the same thing in exactly the same manner every day for the past month. But he was so extremely pleasant about it, so obviously at pains to conquer his timidity in an effort to be friendly, so genuinely concerned for my comfort in a strange land, that I felt no resentment at being obliged to answer for the thirtieth time :

" Yes, very hot ; but I like it."

His smile widened, and he bowed himself away backwards with a " Hoh ! So ! I—am—glad."

The bell rang.

Punctuality would have been unkind, so I set

myself to sip my tea. The cup was inscribed
with my name in Japanese Kata-Kana, a script
specially employed for foreign words :

ド Do-ré-ku ; that being the nearest
レ phonetic approach to Drake. The cup
｜ was decorated, too, with a sprawling
ク image of Daruma, an Indian mystic
who sat so long in contemplation that his legs
rotted beneath him. Truculent, unshaved, with
cloak gathered jealously about him and fly-
switch in hand—and with such a reputation—he
seemed to me an excellent symbol of my own
profession. Also possibly a warning.

The teachers began to file out. I provided
myself with two pieces of chalk and the class
register. It bore the name of the class upon it in
Japanese and English : L 2 B. Which meant,
The Faculty of Law and Literature, second year,
B class. The B class were the literature students,
the A class the law students. I preferred the B.
They were more cheerful, more tractable, more
easily pleased, less under the shadow of an
austere vocation. Nice fellows, if ineffective.
We understood each other.

The class-room was up two flights of stairs ;
an added labour. As I entered, the monitor
called the class to attention :

" *Kirits !* "

I stepped on to the dais and stood to attention too behind my desk.

The monitor called the class to bow :

" *Ré !* "

I bowed in acknowledgment.

I opened the register and called the roll. At certain names a titter went round the room. But the titter meant two different things. In some cases it was a candid enjoyment of my mispronunciation, in others it was a furtive amusement at an absent student's name being successfully answered for him. But I had learnt to distinguish. Quite apart from the tone being different, the first kind was chronic, the second occasional. However, I marked the register according to the answers received, though a simple sum of addition and subtraction showed me that two absent students had been recorded present. But that was merely preparing for a little comic relief when the atmosphere needed cheering.

I glanced at the blackboard, a long affair fixed to the wall behind me. At this a roar of laughter broke out. I saw exactly what I had expected to see. Some one had written :

Dear teacher, too hot day sorry can not work please tell me funny story.

I altered this to :

Dear students, too hot day sorry can not tell funny story too hard work.

This simple sally was greeted by immense applause, which became almost deafening when I proceeded to correct the punctuation and the grammar. It was easy to detect who had written the request by the way in which a single youth covered his face with his hands.

The Eastern mind is delightfully amenable to amusement.

The class was now in perfect good humour, and when the translation was given to them—dictated by one of the boys—they set to work without further demur.

I allowed them twenty-five minutes.

I sat down, and for a little gently simmered.

Then I glanced through the register. It was an extremely efficient document, with the names printed down one side both in Japanese and English, and with columns to mark the absentees for every period. Best of all, on the front page was a chart showing exactly where each student should sit. By checking this with the empty desks it was simple to discover who the two absentees were. Then I glanced through a translation of the business letter, written on the reverse side of the paper by one of the Japanese teachers at the time of the examination. It was an order for an English-Japanese Dictionary, published by a certain firm, and advertised in the Osaka Asahi Shimbun (newspaper) ; it was requested that the dictionary should be sent quickly, and a cheque for ten yen was enclosed to cover cost and postage. Quite a simple little epistle. It was necessary to correct a few mistakes in the translation, to jot down alternative phrases. That exhausted the possibilities of occupation. I had a quarter of an hour to dream away before calling on the students to read their work.

They bent over their papers, writing laboriously, with continual erasings. They sat at separate desks, nearly forty of them, similarly dressed in thin grey-blue summer uniforms : semi-military tunics, and trousers. Their tunic collars were mostly unbuttoned, showing damp brown chests. They carried towels at their hips. Some had their hair cropped, some wore it in long black locks that fell to their shoulders ; the latter wilder spirits with ideas on freedom. They nibbled the ends of pens, consulted one another, consulted dictionaries, their faces drawn in effort and perplexity. One or two had already given up the attempt, and were frankly reading books. Another was fast asleep with his arms thrown over his desk and his head fallen forward. Occasionally one rose, went to a corner of the room and expectorated into a spittoon. Those by the windows were saved the labour of the walk, the windows being open. They blew their noses into pieces of paper, screwing the papers into balls and depositing them in their desks.

I could single out a few whose names I knew : the particularly bright ones, the particularly dull ones, those who visited me at my lodging. But for the most part they were nameless to me. I met nearly two hundred and fifty of them, many only once a week. Dressed alike, and with nothing to individualize their foreign faces except the length of their hair, I found them as indistinguishable as so many poodles. I could never remember their names. And they knew it, making it quite simple for them to answer for each other. But I had learnt how to deal with that.

I began to philosophize ; it was inevitable. Seeing them wrestling with this Western language, which they would never master, which barely one in a hundred would ever use, oppressed too by the burden of the scorching air, I was in the mood to resent the monstrous futility of modern education. I remembered those two books, being studied now in other rooms by other classes : " Life's Little Ironies," " Justice." I can never resist the implication of a symbol. I couldn't resist it then. That the East, set through the centuries to an age-long rigidity, should be forced to run itself into our ephemeral Western mould—was it justice, was it irony ? And that I, who thought myself free of delusions, should be caught into the tragic farce, what was that ? . . .

The twenty-five minutes had passed. I rose, and in an already established formula said :

" Well, we'll go through this now."

They leant back with a unanimous sigh. One or two complained :

" Not yet feeneesh."

" Please, more time."

" Veree dee-fee-cult."

" Very easy," I contradicted.

At which they cried :

" Naw ! Naw ! "

I pretended to look down my mark-book, and called on one of the absentees to read what he had written. The class laughed appreciatively, having known well what was coming, and enjoying the expected in the manner of children. As no one replied I said :

" Ah, he isn't here," and recorded the absence in the register.

Then I called on the other absentee. His friend who had answered for him made an effort at bluff, rising and reading his own composition. This was a new ruse, and the babel of laughter which greeted it made it quite impossible to hear a word.

" I'm sorry," I said, " but I can't understand. I must ask some one else to read."

Then, examining the chart in the register to find out who had just read, I called upon the student by his own name. The counter-ruse was received with a tumultuous delight altogether indescribable. The discomfited student collapsed with his face in his arms while the class cheered uproariously, and even the sleeper awoke and looked about him with filmy eyes. I called upon the sleeper. . . .

By the time peace was restored there remained perhaps a quarter of an hour to go through the translation.

Eventually I singled out a youth who with many stammerings and exclamations, and much scratching of the head and clearing of the throat, produced the following, which I wrote to his dictation word by word upon the board :

P

Keijo
Honmachi
Ichome 3, No. 2
Top day of February, 1928

My dear Company,

How are your shop? Please forget my long silence. I am very sorry to say that I hope you to send me an English-Japanese Dictionary which was established from your shop and was advertisemented in Osaka Asahi Newspaper before sometime ago, to my present domicile of above mentioned hurry up, and I envelope ten yen's cheque for the book's price and the post's pain. I want to be done well.

Your affectionate fellow,
A. MATSUSHIMA

I stook back so that the class could see what I had written, and asked for criticisms and alterations. They studied the composition gravely, their hilarity subsided. They saw in it no cause for amusement. To them it was an entirely serious piece of writing, though somehow not quite tallying with what they read in English books.

Little by little they were emboldened to make suggestions, which I also wrote on the board—there was ample room—grouping them together in this fashion:

Dear you	How are you all?
Dear people	I pray your health!
My dear shoppers	May your Company be blessed!

The following place of mine
The upper abode
The next existence

As soon as this letter has been reached
Very hasty
As fast as can

As a reward here is ten yen
For a ransom and posted tax
I send ten yen as the atonement

Waiting your kindly
Please deal with this as you wish, I hope.

I now had five minutes left in which to explain that such expressions as " How are you all ? " and " May your Company be blessed ! " were inappropriate in a business letter, that such terms as " the next existence " and " the upper abode " were inapplicable to one's terrestrial address, that such words as " reward," " ransom," " atonement," were unsuitable for the purposes of purchase and sale, and that in commercial transactions such confidence as " please deal with this as you wish " and such frankness as " I want to be done well " were, to say the least, indiscreet. I had five minutes in which to explain all this and, moreover, to recast the letter in clear and accurate English. The bell caught me still floundering.

The monitor called the class to attention :
" *Kirits !* "

To bow :

" *Ré !* "

I tucked the register under my arm and left the room.

For ten minutes I was free. The boy-san served me with another cup of hot tea. My two colleagues came to me to be extricated from further difficulties ; but there was no one to extricate me from mine.

Once again the bell rang. The whole performance must be repeated with the A class. But they were dignified and arrogant. The prospect was not so pleasing. However, it was the last period of the day.

A TEMPLE FANTASY

XVIII

THE DIAMOND MOUNTAINS

I AM not attempting to foist off on you some fable of Sindbad the Sailor, though these mountains might readily inspire one to add a chapter to those magical adventures, for here is the same peculiar atmosphere of fantastic fascination, of monstrous enchantment, which lays its compelling spell upon the imagination in the old romance. Yet with the added power of being wrought into reality, acute to the physical senses, without fortfeiting its dark, strange quality of "gramarye." To climb among these incredible peaks is to recapture the visions of childhood, to set chiming again, as it were, the old bells of expectation and wonder. It is to feel once more the ancient wizardry of things ; to feel it, not merely as a response of the spirit, but as an unnamable intoxication of the blood and the bones.

On the Manmulcho, the Peak of the Ten Thousand Resemblances, you look about you, suspended, as it seems, in a point in mid-air, on a semicircle of stark summits which in spite of reason take on strange shapes like living things, beasts and birds, Buddhas in meditation, priests in prayer. Or rather, not like living things ; for with the evening falling, or with a mist drawing over in wisps and veils, the white rocks show wraith-like and insubstantial, surrounding you as though by a company of ghosts. And on the central summit of the Pirobong. . . .

But perhaps you resent being spirited without preparation into the middle of things. You want longitude and latitude as guarantees of actuality, and details of trains and roads. In short, where are these mountains, and how does one get there ?

You will find them on the east of Korea, reaching almost to the sea. A seven-hours' train journey from the capital will take you to the port of Wonsan (Gensan), where you may either take the public motor service or hire a private car for the hundred and fifty odd miles of road which leads to Onjongni (Onseiri) at the opening of the mountains. In two years' time, perhaps less, you will be able to do the whole distance by rail. You will save yourself a great deal of discomfort and a certain hazard, but you will sacrifice an experience. A hundred and fifty miles by car doesn't sound particularly formidable. But you must reckon with the road.

Also, if you elect to travel by the public service, this being cheaper, you must reckon with the car. A Ford, of course ; nothing else could make such a passage. It will be provided with an extra middle bench, thinly upholstered, four inches in width. Avoid it, and make for the back seat, though to attain this you must climb over the wheel. There will be nine people in the car, excluding children. There will be no room for you to stretch your legs, nor, when once settled, for you to shift your position and ease your limbs. And the journey lasts seven hours. Luggage will be corded to the foot-boards, to the radiator, exposed to mud, to streams that you must plunge through, to the weather. So choose your time, in early summer before the rains begin, or, better still, in autumn when the rains are well over. But if you are obliged to make your visit in the middle of the rainy season—as I was—pray for a dry day. And may your prayer avail you. Mine didn't.

Suppose I tell you of my own journey. I was accompanied by a German friend and his wife. As we were already established at the foreign holiday resort at Wonsan we could choose our day. But it was August, a month of alternate blaze and deluge. We decided to start on the first morning that promised possible weather.

But after several mornings of grey cloud that brought no rain we became impatient, and somewhat foolishly set off beneath an uncertain sky. Half an hour after we had started the rain came. The road, cut in a winding ledge round the slopes of steep hills, was almost entirely unmetalled. Within five minutes it became a track of smooth mud, as slippery as ice. There were no chains on the tyres. The car refused to answer the helm. It plunged for the bank, for the precipice, advanced in edging rushes, took the corners at a slide. The driver, revolving an ineffective wheel as though spinning a top, declined to slacken speed. We looked over into rocky gorges, into flooded rice-fields, while the occasional pedestrians fled at our approach, scrambling up banks and along the dikes of paddies. In the valleys streams crossed our path. The rains had swollen them to torrents, undermining the bridges, and carrying them piecemeal away. Uprights corded together in bundles stood forlornly up from the water with loose planks clinging to them and detached posts jutting out at crazy angles. At such places we abandoned the road and jolted down into the river, while stones rattled against the wheels and the engine hissed. It was unnerving. But it was even more unnerving to find a bridge still standing. The torrent beds were infinitely preferable to these lurching causeways gaping with holes. Yet the rain ceased, and the sun came out, drying the road as though at a single hot breath. The mountains loomed more mightily before us, with flying clouds about their summits. We made Onjongni in the evening, driving into the mouth of a tremendous valley brimmed with mist.

Strenuous days followed : to the Nine Dragon Falls, to the Manmulcho, down to the sea where the islands, pine-crested, stood up from the transparent green water in miniature imitation of the inland peaks. The hotel provided us with a guide, who carried our lunch, our rain-coats and a supply of native straw sandals to tie over our boots. An excellent contrivance. Shod so one could stand without fear of slipping on the steepest slopes, though of smooth rock and running with water. The heights were no great matter. But to the eye height is relative. The ravines were cloven so abruptly between the precipitous ranges that the effect was of towering and unscalable summits. Yet one was speedily at the crest. But here magnitude was of no moment. The charm was in other things. In the falls, the chutes, the torrents, alternately a-foam among the boulders and tamed into placid pools, coloured to jade and amber, ice-cold and crystal-clear ; in the groves of pine and maple from which sudden stark faces of rock emerged laced over with threads of crossing water ; in the needle-points of the crests like the columns of fallen temples, like the fingers of gigantic hands ; in the welter of tumbled boulders forming caves, forming gateways, and the peculiar eye-like openings piercing clean through the ridges, showing them as steep and thin as walls ; and farther inland in the innumerable temples, red among the grey and green, set on perilous ledges, seeming to grow from the naked cliffs. Moreover, it was all possessible. It had all that the heart hungered for of wildness and enchantment, but not on too overpowering a scale. It did not daunt one into a mere awed eye-worship. It challenged one to vigorous intimacies. It was assailable without need of forbidding preparations. Yet it demanded a price. The healthy price of effort and endurance and a braced will. For the summits were not conquered without hazard. One mounted by channels of loose boulders, by water-slides, by narrow funnels, skirting by precipitous gorges on cracks in the rock no wider than one's foot. And on the top one stood as though on a column, with the wind pressing and the moving clouds

IN THE DIAMOND MOUNTAINS

making the earth reel, looking down upon the points of rocks like impaling stakes in some vast pit, or on to the spear-like tips of pines. In the rainy season, too, there was the added menace that a sudden shower would swell the torrents impassably, imprisoning one for a day, for a week, in some naked angle of cliff.

Possessible ; but only to the fit and the fearless. But I will not pretend to a courage I do not possess. I have a stupid head for heights. There were places where I held back while my friend pressed after the guide. And one particular moment I still recall with a certain sickening dismay. The mist had caught us on the Manmulcho. We might have returned, but our intention had been to cross the great range and descend by a farther valley. The guide reasoned with us, but we held to our intention. In the thickening mist the peaks about us showed like clouds, like shadows, vanished. Vision became limited to the few paces ahead. In the white opacity we seemed to be following along the crest of a knife-edge ridge. And then of a sudden the guide halted. In front of us was a complete blankness ; a complete blankness to either side. The boulder on which we stood might have been suspended in an emptiness of space. We turned on our tracks ; but where I had been walking upright I now went on my hands and knees. . . .

Pushing more deeply into the mountains one comes to Changansa (Choanji). From here one can make excursions to the temples and the monasteries ; for Buddhism has claimed these mountains as its own particular domain. One is regaled with fanciful legends of the coming of the Fifty-Three Buddhas in a stone ship from the Land of Wulchi, and of their battles with the griffins of the rocks and the dragons of the pools, till gradually the land was rid of its monsters and claimed for the worship of Amida. Quite childish legends, yet pregnant with significance. Possibly there are still tigers in the mountains, and there are certainly bears ; and looking into the whirling waters one can image them to the scaly coils of dragons. The earlier monks must have had a hard struggle to maintain themselves against the beasts and the floods and the weather, and it must have seemed to them that they were pitted against savage and antagonistic forces ranged against them in deliberate hostility. Perhaps they were right. For the challenge of Buddhism, like the challenge of Christianity, is to the Spirit of the Ancient Earth. And here in these mountains the challenge seems to have been carried into the

THE HANGING TEMPLE, THE DIAMOND MOUNTAINS

very stronghold of the Spirit. Buddhism appears to have triumphed. The temples are there and the monasteries without number ; not in the valleys, but perched as though in defiance on the steepest cliffs. In particular the Hanging Temple near Makayun seems to be suspended from an outcropping rock overlooking a deep abyss. Yet one wonders if the triumph is complete. The temples are painted, not only with Buddha and his disciples, but with a menagerie of strange beasts, as though admitting to its worship, or to its philosophy, the forces it has set itself to conquer. Moreover, the legends which tell of the routing of the dragons do not seem to claim their complete extinction. Many were killed, but some escaped, fleeing for shelter to the inner recesses of the mountains.

I saw their retreat.

That was when I stood upon the summit of the Pirobong, the highest of the peaks. I was parted from my friend now. At Changansa I found an English-speaking guide. He led me up a magnificent ravine to the Hanging Temple, and from there to a monastery rest-house at the foot of the Pirobong. It was still early afternoon, and I proposed climbing the peak straight away. My guide declared it was impossible. We could never return by nightfall, and to be caught in the dark would be to lay ourselves open to unnamable perils. I wasn't to be put off so. I was in perfect trim now after a week or more in the mountains, and to idle for an afternoon was intolerable. Besides, I knew the fellow was lying. His aping of foreign dress proclaimed him untrustworthy. He wore a cotton vest, a pair of khaki breeches unlaced at the knees, no stockings, and Japanese *tabi*, a short sock-like foot-gear split at the big toe like mittens, which gave a cloven-hoofed appearance to his feet. Apart from this sartorial medley, he had an amiably insinuating manner of recounting his country's legends as though deriding them as fables fit for children but beneath the intelligence of a superior man who could " speakee " English. But though I knew he was lying I was at some pains to discover the motive of the lie. Yet I stumbled upon it at last. I had walked so quickly, it seemed, that I had covered a day's stage in a morning, and now I was proposing to cover another day's stage in the afternoon. My guide would be doing two days' work for a day's fee. I learnt further that there was a sort of trade union among the guides—among the superior ones, at least, who could speak English—they had portioned out the mountains into stages to which visitors must submit. Well, I had merely

THE GREAT BUDDHA, THE DIAMOND MOUNTAINS

to offer a double fee to be told that if we walked very quickly we might just be able to return before nightfall. We did so without difficulty.

There was no mist that day, not so much as a single cloud. We passed by a gigantic Buddha— forty feet in height, it was said—hewn in the solid rock. We turned aside into a maple wood, following up a stream, where chipmunks peeped from the branches and kingfishers dived in the pools. We emerged into a steep and naked gorge of boulders, where, free of the trees, we had suddenly in view the ragged edge of the granite crest looming up above us in a silhouette of an almost chalky whiteness against the intense blue vault of the sky.

Reaching the summit, we looked round upon the whole formation of the mountains, tracing the valleys and distinguishing the peaks. Everything showed in a stark, detached clarity. Fifteen miles away, yet seeming to lie at our feet, was the sea, minutely patterned with waves, with the coastline spread out like a painted map, bays of golden sand between green and purple headlands reaching a hundred miles to either hand. And immediately below us, at an almost sheer drop, as it seemed, of several thousand feet, was an enormous valley, or basin rather, enclosed by naked, precipitous walls of cliff.

Across this basin my guide indicated for me a summit where the head waters began of the Nine Dragon Falls. It might have been three miles away. Yet after visiting the Falls I had been obliged to make a two-days' circuit to reach the Pirobong. Why? I put the question to my guide. Couldn't one cut across the valley below? He seemed to be taken with a sort of trembling. No one could go that way, he said. Once there was a path, known only to an ancient priest. But that was a long time ago, and now the priest was dead. Many people had tried to open the way again ; but they didn't return. Only a few weeks since a party had set out. But they also, they didn't return. . . . The place was haunted. It was "faerie." For I remembered the dragons who had fled for shelter to the inner recesses of the mountains. This was their lair, and they were potent still. . . .

The city had been fretful with ephemeral antagonisms : Japan and Korea, East and West. But here a fundamental struggle was engaged : the temples against the mountains, human pities and solaces and dreams against the relentless reality of the Ancient Earth. A reality the more vital for that sense in it of a dark wonder, yet steadying, fortifying. And, as for me, I was on the side of the mountains.

On the side of the mountains, in spite of my stupid head. For I thought I had glimpsed a flying revelation of the Truth. We were natives of the rocks and the waters, not intruders from the skies. The common earth sufficed for us. Truth lay, not in rebellion, not in abnegation, but in a passionate acceptance of necessity. And in the light of such a vision life became worth living ; not for any statable purpose, but purely for the sake of being alive. Joy was its own justification, endeavour its own goal. And that, instead of fluctuant doubts, was something positive and reliable. . . .

But down in the city again the vision faded. One was taken in the old fatuities, alternately buffeted and becalmed amid puerile contentions, like a passenger on some unprofitable voyage, bound, you might say, on an ocean of Nothingness for the port of Nowhere.

However, that was only in the city. The mountains had declared otherwise. And they had spoken with authority.

THE END

Q

BY THE SAME AUTHOR

THE SCHOONER CALIFORNIA

7s. 6d. net

"The Author creates an atmosphere of uncanny mystery and maintains it without loss of tension right to the end; against this background his characters stand out extraordinarily vividly, and he is to be congratulated on having produced what is perhaps the best story of its kind since Conrad's 'Rescue.'"
—*Manchester Guardian.*

"So impressively conceived, and developed with so rich a detail . . . make no mistake about it—it is a very fine story."
—*Morning Post.*

"It is a joy to welcome and commend 'The Schooner California.'"—*Observer.*

"There is something decidedly Stevensonian in this sea story. . . . We hope Mr. Drake will do it again."
—*Daily Chronicle.*

"A gorgeous story of adventure."—GERALD GOULD in the
—*Daily News.*

"A rousing story of adventure by sea and land, with real thrills in it, is something to be grateful for, and Mr. H. B. Drake has earned our gratitude, and more than that."
John O'London's Weekly.

JOHN LANE THE BODLEY HEAD LTD., VIGO STREET, W.1

CURSED BE THE TREASURE

"Readers of Mr. H. B. Drake's previous admirable story, 'The Schooner California,' will not be disappointed in this. It is a tale of hidden treasure that brought doom and death to all who sought it. It is a stirring tale, very well written. It belongs to the Stevensonian tradition, but the Author is no mere imitator. He has a method and style of his own."

John O'London's Weekly.

THE CHILDREN REAP

"Mr. H. B. Drake is already familiar to the public as a romantic writer of exceptionally high quality, and this story gives us another thoughtful, well-written, and enthralling study of the heroic and the uncanny."—*Times Literary Supplement.*

SHINJU

"It is very convincing, with a touch of Marlowe-esque splendour about it. . . . He succeeds in giving the reader intimate glimpses into the very soul of that people so different from the people of the West. The descriptions of the external life of Japan are exquisitely pictorial."—*Everyman.*

JOHN LANE THE BODLEY HEAD LTD., VIGO STREET, W.I